PRAISE FOR JACKSON DEAN CHASE

— USA TODAY BESTSELLING AUTHOR —

AS SEEN IN

BUZZFEED AND THE HUFFINGTON POST

"[Jackson Dean Chase is] a fresh and powerful new voice."
— Terry Trueman, Printz Honor author of *Stuck in Neutral*

"[Chase] grabs readers from page one."
— Nate Philbrick, author of *The Little One*

"[Jackson Dean Chase] succeeds in taking fiction to a whole new level."
— TheBaynet.com

"[Jackson's fiction is] diligently crafted..."
— The Huffington Post

"Irresistible... [Jackson knows how to write] a heart-pounding story full of suspense, romance, and action!"
— Buzzfeed

ALSO BY JACKSON DEAN CHASE

FAST, FUN ADVICE FOR BUSY AUTHORS

ULTIMATE AUTHOR'S GUIDE: OMNIBUS 1

A MASTERCLASS IN WRITING DYNAMITE STORY HOOKS AND CHARACTERS

JACKSON DEAN CHASE

WWW.JACKSONDEANCHASE.COM

First printing, October 2018

ISBN-13: 978-1727833188 / ISBN-10: 172783318X

Published by Jackson Dean Chase, Inc.

ULTIMATE AUTHOR'S GUIDE: OMNIBUS 1

PUBLISHER'S NOTE

FOREWORD

WHAT'S INSIDE AND WHY IT WILL HELP

This special omnibus collects the first two volumes of *The Ultimate Author's Guide* series: *Writing Dynamite Story Hooks* and *Writing Heroes and Villains*. Although there are plenty of nods to speculative fiction, this is universal info any author can use regardless of genre or literary aspirations, and it applies whether you write for adults, teens, or kids.

My books have helped thousands of authors, from beginner to advanced. No matter where you are in your writer career, the information is easy to understand and easy to learn. There is no fluff or filler, no boring anecdotes. Those aren't the kind of books I like or can learn from, so that's not the kind of book I write.

And when I say "easy to learn," I also mean *fun to read*. I want my writing guides to feel like a casual conversation between us. So lean back and let's talk about how to write bestselling fiction!

— JACKSON DEAN CHASE
USA TODAY Bestselling Author
Get a FREE BOOK at www.JacksonDeanChase.com

P.S.: As I mentioned before, the contents of the books contained in this omnibus were previously published as:

- *Writing Dynamite Story Hooks*
- *Writing Heroes & Villains*

I just want to point out that they are reprinted here exactly as they appear in their current, individual editions. It's also worth noting that the content of these books originally appeared in a different form as:

- *How to Start Your Novel*
- *How to Write Realistic Characters*
- *How to Write Realistic Men*
- *How to Write Realistic Women*

These books were all revised and updated when they became part of *The Ultimate Author's Guide* series.

P.P.S.: Want more of my writing secrets? The second omnibus in this series focuses on science fiction, fantasy, horror, and related subgenres like post-apocalyptic fiction.

ULTIMATE AUTHOR'S GUIDE: OMNIBUS 1

WRITING DYNAMITE STORY HOOKS

A MASTERCLASS IN FICTION + MEMOIR

"Your first line sells the book. Your last line sells the next book."

— MICKEY SPILLANE, AUTHOR OF KISS ME DEADLY

PREFACE

WELCOME, FRIEND, to the *Ultimate Author's Guide to Writing Dynamite Story Hooks*. This is an expanded edition of my breakthrough bestseller, *How to Start your Novel*, with new ways to hook readers, new story secrets, and even more examples from the greatest authors of yesterday and today.

How much new stuff is there? Well, this edition is *fifty pages longer* than the first, so I'd say a lot! I've increased the number of successful ways to begin your story from seven to ten, restored original material cut for space, and included examples for all these genres:

- Crime/Hardboiled/*Noir*
- Fantasy
- Historical Fiction
- Memoir
- Mystery/Suspense/Thriller
- Romance
- Science Fiction
- Young Adult

This book covers the top 10 ways successful authors hook readers.

All smart, powerful stuff. I lay it all out for you in *easy to learn examples* with a fun, casual tone in my comments. The first things we'll cover is how to hook with:

1. Action
2. Dialogue
3. Hero or Sidekick
4. Meeting
5. Monologue
6. Mystery
7. Premonition
8. Profound Statement
9. Setting
10. Villain or Victims

After you learn the top 10 ways to hook readers, we're going to cover the top 10 ways to lose readers:

1. Antiquated Writing Style, Foreign Language, or Technobabble
2. Correspondence or Diary
3. Dream or Flashback
4. Nothing Happens
5. Phone Call
6. Prologue or Frame
7. Telling or Info-Dumping
8. Unlikable or Flat Hero
9. Waking Up
10. Weather

I know some of you are stubborn and will want to use the "wrong ways" no matter what. That's why I'm going to show you *how to break the rules* and make the wrong ways work. When you add the fixed versions, you're really getting *twice as many* successful hooks!

WHO IS THIS BOOK FOR?

This is book is for anyone serious about the craft of writing fiction—from short stories to novels, even memoir. Which reminds me, the memoir section has been *totally revised and expanded*, making it much more useful to nonfiction authors. It even has ideas for celebrity memoirs—and ideas you can take from them to write your own.

There's another added benefit to expanding the memoir section: Because most memoirs begin with interior monologue, this essentially *doubles* the number of ideas and excerpts for how novelists can hook fiction readers with their characters' thoughts and feelings.

YEARS OF EXPERIENCE

At this point in my career, I've written over thirty books, won and been nominated for multiple awards, and hit the *USA TODAY* bestseller list. *Writing Dynamite Story Hooks* condenses all my years of experience into one fun to read, easy to learn from guide—a "masterclass" I know will inspire you to write bestsellers of your own.

Being an author is my dream and I'm living it.

It's a hell of a ride.

Now it's your turn. Take the journey with me.

Do it.

Do it now.

Don't look back.

— JACKSON DEAN CHASE
www.JacksonDeanChase.com

PLEASE LEAVE A REVIEW

If you enjoy this book, please leave a review to help others in their author journey.

INTRODUCTION

DO YOU KNOW THE SECRET?

THE FIRST WORDS ON THE PAGE are the hardest you'll ever write. It's easy to get overwhelmed by choices. How do bestselling authors do it? That's what I set out to discover. I tore apart my library, scouring the openings to hundreds of my favorite novels and short stories to see what makes them work and why. And do you know what I found? A pattern—a secret formula authors use time and time again to deliver powerful, bestselling results. And do you know what else?

- *Genre doesn't matter.*
- *Point of view doesn't matter.*
- *It works for novels, novellas, and short stories.*
- *It works for series or standalone books.*
- *It even works for memoirs.*

SO WHAT IS THE SECRET FORMULA?

The secret is in the story's opening line and how you construct it to "hook" readers into wanting more. A story hook is a literary technique that grabs readers' attention. Usually, the hook is in the first line, but sometimes it's in the second. More rarely, it only becomes evident after reading the first paragraph or two. It depends on the story the author is telling and what effect they're trying to achieve. The longer you delay your hook, the more likely readers are to stop reading, so never delay your hook longer than necessary!

The formula in this book will teach you how to write killer hooks —the kind that get noticed by agents, editors, and readers. My formula contains ten sure-fire ways successful authors use to open their stories and ten ways unsuccessful authors use.

Were there exceptions? Of course, but I quickly found the pattern and unlocked that secret formula too. I learned that in skilled hands, some of the wrong ways can actually be turned into the right ways (but it's tricky, and not always done the way you think).

In this breakthrough book, I'm going to reveal all these secrets and more in an unbeatable quick and dirty system that will take your writing to the next level. I break down how and why each way succeeds or fails with clear examples from bestselling fiction that show you how the formula works.

How to Write Dynamite Story Hooks is an easy to read, easy to use toolkit designed to be your "go to" guide every time you start a new story. Let's face it: in today's tough market, we all need an edge.

This book is the *secret weapon* you've been waiting for!

— Jackson Dean Chase

P.S.: "Fair Use" law prevents me from quoting more than roughly 300 or so words from another author's copyrighted material, so although I may quote from multiple books by the same author, I've been forced to limit how much I quote from any one source.

This sometimes results in me skipping over one or more paragraphs to get to the part that's most relevant to making my point. Whenever this occurs, I call it out in the text or use ellipses (...). Otherwise, even when broken up by my commentary, the scenes play out exactly as they do in the source material.

P.P.S.: Note that the case studies from the first edition have been removed to make room for exciting new material. Maybe they'll return in a companion book someday...

I

THE TEN WAYS EVERY STORY
SHOULD BEGIN

Learn by example with inspiring excerpts
from bestselling authors

ACTION

THE NUMBER ONE WAY to open a genre book is with action, but be careful how you set it up. You can't jump into a fight scene before you introduce your hero.[1] No one knows him, so no one cares what happens to him. So how do you do it?

Announce the action is taking place and place the enemy close, but not too close. This allows you to get your hero's reaction to the danger, providing valuable insight into who they are, where they are, and what they are up to when the action occurs:

> Logen plunged through the trees, bare feet slipping and sliding on the wet earth, the slush, the wet pine needles, breath rasping in his chest, blood thumping in his head.
>
> — JOE ABERCOMBIE, THE BLADE ITSELF

This is a prime example of how to open *in media res* (Latin for "in the middle of things"). Who is Logen? We know he's in a forest, struggling to escape, but from what? Let's see how bestselling grimdark fantasy author Joe Abercrombie handles it in his complete opening paragraph:

> Logen plunged through the trees, bare feet slipping and sliding on the wet earth, the slush, the wet pine needles, breath rasping in his chest, blood thumping in his head. He stumbled and sprawled onto his side, nearly cut his chest open on his own axe, lay there panting, peering through the shadow forest.

We learn Logen has an axe, so whatever he's running from is more than he and his weapon can handle. We also pay off the potential danger of his "bare feet slipping and sliding" from the first sentence by making Logen fall in the second. That lets us know Logen is not invincible, nor is he immune to fear or accidents.

Abercrombie has efficiently *humanized* his hero right from the start by showing, not telling.[2] If he'd simply told us Logen was afraid, that would have been lazy writing. Instead, he shows us through internal and external sensory details. The fast, choppy style conveys panic. As a result, readers can empathize with Logen. The only problem is, we don't know much about him. That's where the second paragraph comes in:

> The Dogman had been with him until a moment before, he was sure, but there wasn't any sign of him now. As for the others, there was no telling. Some leader, getting split up from the boys like that. He should've been trying to get back, but the Shanka were all around. He could feel them moving between the trees, his nose was full of the smell of them. Sounded as if there was some shouting somewhere on his left, fighting maybe. Logen crept slowly to his feet, trying to stay quiet. A twig snapped and he whipped around.

This second paragraph tells us everything else we need to know: Logen is the leader of a band of fighting men, and he has not willingly abandoned them, but been split off during a retreat from a superior force. This deepens reader empathy. The hero is not a coward, simply unlucky. Everyone can relate to that.

In the next few paragraphs, Logen is attacked by two of the Shanka and we see how well he fights. But the author does not let this happen before we get a sense of who his hero and his allies are, where they are, and what's going on. That is critical to the success of not only the book, but the author, and why he received reviews like, "You'd never guess that *The Blade Itself* is Joe Abercrombie's first novel. He writes like a natural."

The Blade Itself opens with the hero already in motion and the bad guys hot on his tail.

Here's another example, this time from a science fiction perspective:

Death came for him through the trees.

— STEVE PERRY, THE MAN WHO NEVER MISSED

You can't get better than that. In a single, powerful sentence, we know the hero is in a forest and in terrible danger. From there, the author fills us in on what the danger is:

It came in the form of a tactical squad, four people walking three-and-one, the point followed by the tight concave arc; the optimum number in the safest configuration. It was often said the Confed's military was always training to fight the last war and it was true enough, only there had been enough last wars to give them sand or cold or jungle troops as needed. These four were jungle-trained, they wore class-one shiftsuits with viral/molecular computers able to match backgrounds within a quarter second; they carried .177 Parkers, short and brutal carbines which held five hundred rounds of explosive ammo—one man could put down a half-meter-thick tree with two waves of his weapon on automatic. The quad carried heat sensors, com-implants, Doppler gear and personal sidearms; they were the deadliest and best-equipped soldiers the Confed could field and they were good. They moved through the cool rain forest quietly and efficiently, alert for any signs of the Shanda Scum. If something moved, they were going to spike it, hard.

From the second paragraph[3], we know this is a sci-fi story, we know the "evil empire" is called the Confed, and they have been at war a long time. We also get a sense of the technology available to them and who they are hunting for (rebel scum). All good stuff, but we still don't know who the hero is. That's fine, because Steve Perry skillfully provides that information in the third paragraph:

> Khadaji felt the fear in himself, the familiar coldness in the pit of his belly, an old and unwelcome tenant. He had learned to live with it, it was necessary, but he was never comfortable when it came to this. He took a deeper breath and pressed his back harder against the rough bark of the sumwin tree. He practiced invisibility. The tree was three meters thick, they couldn't see him, and even without his confounder gear their directional doppler and heat sensors wouldn't read through that much solid wood. He listened as they moved past him. The soft ferns brushed against the shiftsuits of the quad; the humus of a thousand years made yet softer sounds under their slippers as they walked, but Khadaji knew exactly where they were when he stepped away from the tree.

You can guess what happens next: Khadaji assassinates the entire quad. After all, the name of the book is *The Man Who Never Missed*.

But what if you want to open with your hero *before* the bad guys are actively hunting her? This next example shows how to do that:

> The attack came in the hour before dawn. The girl woke to the stench of burning thatch and the sound of her mother screaming.[4] Outside, in the clearing beyond the hut, she heard her father's response, and the clash of iron on bronze. Another man shouted—not her father—and she was up, throwing off the hides, reaching back into the dark behind the sleeping place for her skinning knife or, better, her axe. She found neither. Her mother screamed again, differently. The girl scrabbled frantically, feeling the fire scorch her skin and the sliding ache of fear that was the threat of a sword-cut to the spine. Her fingers closed on a haft of worn wood, running down to the curve of a grip she knew

from hours of oil and polish and the awe of youth; her father's boar spear. She jerked it free, turning and pulling the leather cover from the blade in one move. A wash of predawn light hit her eyes as the door-skin was ripped from its hangings and replaced as rapidly by a shadow. The bulk of a body filled the doorway. Dawn light flickered on a sword blade. Close by, her father screamed her name. *"Breaca!"*

— MANDA SCOTT, DREAMING THE EAGLE

In one paragraph, we know the setting is a primitive village under attack, the time, that the hero is a girl named Breaca who is familiar with weapons, and that she is in danger. Note that the enemy doesn't appear until near the end of the first paragraph. Just long enough to give us the details we need to know *before* the violence begins.

You can pull off the same effect in countless situations, even if you don't begin with action. For example, your hero could be about to play the winning hand in an illegal high-stakes poker game when armed robbers bust in and demand the money. That gives your opening the added advantage of misdirection. The reader thinks he's getting a scene about gambling, then you switch to robbery. The hero goes from winner to loser in a heartbeat, gaining reader empathy in the process.

Sometimes, stories begin with the hero witnessing violence without being involved.

We were about to give up and call it a night when somebody threw the girl off the bridge.

They came to a yelping stop overhead, out of sight, dumped her and took off.

It was a hot Monday night in June. With moon. It was past midnight and just past the tide change. A billion bugs were vectoring in on us as the wind began to die.

It seemed to be a very final way of busting up a romance.

— JOHN D. MACDONALD, DARKER THAN AMBER

There are a ton of questions raised by this intro:

1. Who is the girl?
2. Is she dead or alive?
3. Who threw her off the bridge?
4. *Why* did they throw her?
5. What were the hero and his friend about to give up before they saw the girl thrown from the bridge?

The arrival of enemies doesn't have to bring with it immediate violence. It can merely be the *threat* of violence, the intimidation, indignity, and humiliation enemies bring.

> My used bookstore had been open for just about a month when the police showed up. I hadn't called them, of course; a black man has to think twice before calling the cops in Watts. They came to see me late that afternoon. Two well-built young men. One had dark hair and the other sported freckles.
>
> The dark one wandered around the room, flipping through random books, looking, it seemed, for some kind of contraband.
>
> "Where'd you get all these books, son?" the other cop asked, looking down on me.
>
> I was sitting in my favorite swivel chair behind the makeshift table-desk that I used for book sales and purchases.
>
> "Libraries," I replied.
>
> "Stole 'em?" the dark-haired cop asked from across the room. There was an eager grin on his face.
>
> — WALTER MOSLEY, FEARLESS JONES

There are no swords, no lasers, and nobody's dead (yet) but the threat is real. Menace hangs in the air: menace, bigotry, and hate. The cops are looking to roust the hero just because he's black, and maybe they're looking to do something more besides. A frightening situation, but a fantastic way to hook readers.

But what if it's not action with enemies, but with a natural disaster or some other dangerous survival situation? What do you do then? Pretty much the same thing:

I was thrown out of bed.

— RUDOLPH WURLITZER, QUAKE

It doesn't get simpler than that! The author isn't fooling around and has no intention of wasting our time. He just jumps right in, and that's fine because there's only the hero to focus on and a disaster he can't do anything about. The rest of the opening continues the danger:

The mirror fell off the wall and shattered over the dresser. The floor moved again and the ceiling sagged towards me.

The first paragraph establishes the bedroom and the danger. The second expands the setting and the action, as well as the strange, deadpan reaction the hero has. This tells us we're dealing with a potentially unreliable narrator.

It was dawn and I was in the Tropicana Motel in Los Angeles. There was another trembling through the room and what sounded like wires snapping and windows breaking. Then it was very quiet. I lay back on the floor and shut my eyes. I was in no hurry. There was a high prolonged scream by the pool and then a splash and another, shorter scream. I stood up and raised my arms over my head and tried to touch my toes, an early morning ritual I never perform. The wall next to the bed was moving as if it was alive and I walked into the bathroom.

Another kind of hero would react to in a different manner with the expected panic or bravery. But Wurlitzer isn't interested in normal. His hero does the opposite of what any sane person would do, and that's what makes him interesting. He doesn't care if he lives or dies. Maybe a post-quake world is better than the one before...

Comedy can also work with action to hook readers:

My sister threw down the book she was reading. To be exact, she threw it at me.

— ROBERT E. HOWARD, "THE LITTLE PEOPLE"

Thrown objects are funny, but what about thrown people?

They threw me off the hay truck about noon.

— JAMES M. CAIN, THE POSTMAN ALWAYS RINGS TWICE

Action doesn't have to be violence or fast motion; it can be almost any criminal act:

He always shot up by TV light.

— JAMES ELLROY, AMERICAN TABLOID

Action can imply guilt (or protestations of innocence):

The building was on fire, and it wasn't my fault.

— JIM BUTCHER, BLOOD RITES

Action can show illness or injury:

As Roy Dillon stumbled out of the shop, his face was a sickish green, and each breath he drew was an incredible agony.

— JIM THOMPSON, THE GRIFTERS

Opening with someone hurt, sick, or dying creates sympathy and excitement. Readers become invested in the outcome and want to find out how it happened.

Action can also show surprise and instantly reveal genre:

I was staring out the classroom window when I spotted the flying saucer.

— ERNEST CLINE, ARMADA

Action can also represent a flurry of activity, even if centered around a seemingly normal event:

As the clock ticked down on her senior year in high school, Laurel McBane learned one indisputable fact.
Prom was hell.

— NORA ROBERTS, SAVOR THE MOMENT

Let's come full circle and end this chapter as it began—with violence, but not just any violence. The difference here is the violence is resolved *before* the first sentence:

After the guy was dead and the smell of his burning flesh was off the air, we all went down to the beach.

— STEPHEN KING, "NIGHT SURF"

What kind of sick weirdos would burn a guy to death then go party? If you want to find out, you have to read more, and Stephen King knows that. The rest of his paragraph neatly segues into casually talking about the narrator's friends—normal teenage stuff—but all is not as it seems and the narrator drops clues about a world-ending plague which means there was a good reason to burn that guy after all!

Other than shock value, the advantage to this opening is combining action with mystery. Burning the body creates the action, while the follow-up creates the mystery. Which leads us to the first story secret:

STORY SECRET #1

COMBINING DIFFERENT OPENINGS

Combining different ways to open your story can create all kinds of interesting results. It's an advanced technique, but when you get it right, it's just as valid a way to open as any of the ten ways on their own—perhaps even more so.

Go back and look at the excerpts in this chapter. Notice they didn't just hook with action, but with mystery, like Stephen King did in "Night Surf." Who is Logen running from? What threw the narrator out of bed? Why is Roy Dillon sick? It's a one-two punch!

∽

CHAPTER 1 FOOTNOTES

- 1 I define the word "hero" to mean any gender.
- 2 For more about why telling is a terrible way to open your novel, see Chapter 17: Telling or Info-Dumping.
- 3 This paragraph is a bit long, but gets the job done. Back when *The Man Who Never Missed* was written (1985), longer paragraphs hadn't gone out of fashion yet. If you write something like this now, I recommend breaking it up into shorter paragraphs.
- 4 A hero waking up is normally a bad way to open, but it works here because it's a reaction to danger.

DIALOGUE

LIKE ACTION, when you start with dialogue, you are often *in media res*. Dialogue puts you into the mouth of a character with something brief and important to say. It can't be, "Hello, how are you?" or "Please, sit down." Anything normal is the kiss of death.

Dialogue must be powerful and, like action, it must refer to something exciting that either has happened, is happening, or is about to happen, so make sure there is at least a hint of mystery or danger in your words.

"We should head back," Gared urged as the woods began to grow dark around them. "The wildlings are dead."

— GEORGE R. R. MARTIN, A GAME OF THRONES

Although Gared is a minor character, this third person opening is still an excellent beginning. We get an immediate sense of peril, and know that there has been a battle, yet some greater danger remains. What is it? We cannot help but find out. Also, notice how the author mentions the darkening forest between the dialogue. That helps set the scene... and the danger.

"Do the dead frighten you?" Ser Waymer Royce asked with just the hint of a smile.

Gared did not rise to the bait. He was an old man, past fifty, and he had seen lordlings come and go. "Dead is dead," he said. "We have no business with the dead."

These next paragraphs introduce another minor character, Ser Waymer Royce, and create conflict between him and Gared. They also sketch in a few details about the speakers and their world. More importantly, they both keep talking about the dead.

By placing such importance on them, we begin to feel uneasy. It's getting dark. The men are in a forest. Night is falling. This is a medieval fantasy world, so it stands to reason there are a lot of superstitions about the dead coming back to life, not to mention ghosts, curses, that sort of thing. If you've read the books or seen the HBO show, then you know what I'm talking about.

"Are they dead?" Royce asked softly. "What proof have we?"

"Will saw them," Gared said. "If he says they are dead, that's proof enough for me."

Will had known they would drag him into the quarrel sooner or later. He wished it had been later rather than sooner. "My mother told me that dead men sing no songs," he put in.

The conversation continues, now bringing in a third minor character, Will, who is the hero of this prologue. By saving Will's reveal for last, we get a chance to peer inside his thoughts for a moment before he speaks. This serves two purposes:

1. It breaks up the conversation which helps pacing; and
2. it sheds some light on Will before he ever opens his mouth. By going inside his head and not into the heads of Gared or Royce, we know Will is more important to the story. We establish him as the hero.

Could Will have spoken first? Sure, and that would have been a perfectly valid way to open, but sometimes it's better to hold the hero back so when he does come in, he's already been set up by others, and the situation clearly established. That frees the hero's introduction from unnecessary clutter.

> "We have a long ride ahead of us," Gared pointed out. "Eight days, maybe nine. And night is falling."
>
> Ser Waymer Royce glanced at the sky with disinterest. "It does that every day about this time. Are you unmanned by the dark, Gared?"

Danger is again threatened by the mention of night, then dismissed. It's important to have one character who refuses to heed the warning, who is more interested in scoring points via insults or witty remarks. This creates conflict, but it also ramps up suspense. Reader sympathy shifts to the character(s) who urge caution.

Note that not every question merits a reply, or at least not an immediate one. Some questions lead to monologue instead, with the other characters reflecting on their feelings. It's also a valuable opportunity to weave in more details about the speakers, their world, and their situation. Especially details that have no place in dialogue:

> Will could see the tightness around Gared's mouth, the barely suppressed anger in his eyes under the thick black hood of his cloak. Gared had spent forty years in the Night's Watch, man and boy, and he was not accustomed to being made light of. Yet it was more than that. Under the wounded pride, Will could sense something else in the older man. You could taste it, a nervous tension that came perilous close to fear.

We need Gared's reaction, since he was the one insulted and questioned, but we don't need to jump into Gared's head to get it. By seeing his reaction through Will's eyes, we stress Will's importance and hero status. Gared takes on a mentor role, and Royce continues to be cemented as the immediate villain. We also get more suspense as Will notices Gared's fear.

Since we just established Gared is wise and experienced, we know his advice should be heeded and Royce is a reckless fool likely to get them all killed. But we need more than this; we need Will's reaction. This is deftly supplied by the author in the next paragraph, filling us in on Will's own experiences "beyond the Wall" and why he shares Gared's fear.

After that, we get Will's opinion of Royce as a terrible commanding officer, and then it's back to dialogue as the men argue about what to do next. From there, it's just a few more pages before their worst fears come to life...

You don't need to commit to an entire conversation to have a successful opening. Often, only a line or two is all you need. But pick your words carefully. They must be compelling:

> "Go on," Cressner said again. "Look in the bag."
>
> — STEPHEN KING, "THE LEDGE"

This is a great combination of dialogue and mystery. Cressner is insisting the main character look inside the bag. Knowing this is a Stephen King story, we can already begin to imagine all kinds of horrible things lurking inside.

But rather than continue the conversation as Martin did in the previous example, King opts to describe his setting because, unlike Martin, he could not include that information with-out cluttering up his opening and robbing it of its power. Those details are shifted to the second paragraph:

> We were in his penthouse apartment, forty-three stories up. The carpet was deep-cut pile, burnt orange. In the middle, between the Basque sling chair where Cressner sat and the genuine leather couch where no one at all sat, there was a brown shopping bag.
>
> "If it's a payoff, forget it," I said. "I don't want it."

The room description is kept brief but long enough to accomplish two things:

1. that the apartment is expensively furnished and on the top floor; and
2. that Cressner is sitting, which implies it's his apartment.

After that, we cut back to dialogue to introduce the narrator. Because of the clever way King phrased the empty couch description, we know the narrator is standing in front of Cressner.

As well as providing conflict and raising suspense, the narrator's reply gives insight into his relationship with Cressner. That's about as neat a set-up as anyone could wish for in a story.

Dialogue doesn't have to be serious. Comedy can hook readers just as easily as suspense:

"There they go again," I said. "Two o'clock in the morning, and they're up there running a footrace."

— JIM THOMPSON, "THE THREESOME IN FOUR-C"

The title makes this funny because we know the narrator is talking about loud sex. And speaking of sex, how about this example:

"But you don't really love me," Carla sighed as she pushed Jason's persistent hand from her unsnapped jeans.

— MICHAEL GARRETT, "REUNION"

Carla recognizing Jason can't give her the love she wants tells us a lot more about her in one sentence than a sex scene would in a page.

Why? Because you can't jump into your story with a full-on sex scene anymore than you can with a huge battle. Yes, it's important things move quickly, but not so fast you fail to properly introduce your hero *and* give us a compelling reason to read about her.

You can also use dialogue to shock your reader:

"It's not that I have anything against you personally, Davis," the old man said. "But I simply must kill you."

— CHARLES E. FRITCH, "THE PAWNSHOP"

With an opening line like that, you can bet readers will be hooked. Always lead with your strongest words and you will be miles ahead of most writers. Don't hold back!

STORY SECRET #2

DIALOGUE ISN'T REALLY DIALOGUE

Go back and study the dialogue opening examples again. See anything similar between them? Sure, they all start *in media res*, and yes, they introduce us to characters saying interesting and important things, but they do more than that—they use dialogue as a way to set up one of the other nine ways to start your novel:

- *A Game of Thrones* uses premonition.
- "The Ledge" and "The Pawnshop" use mystery.
- "The Threesome in Four-C" and "Reunion" use action.

Think of dialogue as one of the other nine ways cloaked in stealth mode. Because it's a character delivering the information rather than the author, it's an opportunity to ease a reader in with a "fly on the wall" approach.

All the other ways (with the exception of monologue), create an initial distance between the reader and the story world, a few seconds where the reader has to think about and visualize the situation. The advantage to that is the ability to provide greater clarity but at the expense of those first seconds. Vivid dialogue paints the picture for us.

HERO OR SIDEKICK

ANOTHER WAY TO HOOK READERS is to introduce them to your hero through describing him. This can be done in either in the third person, by a sidekick (especially one who narrates the hero's story, as in *The Great Gatsby*), the villain (Salieri in *Amadeus*) or by the hero himself.

This is very similar to the way villains can be used to hook readers, but of course, the aim here is to make you like the hero, not fear him. If the hero is described by another character, then the aim also becomes for the reader to like that character as well, because it is obvious we are going to be spending a lot of time with them, and the events will be filtered through their eyes, their hopes and fears and hates.

Perhaps the easiest way is to describe your hero in the most straightforward manner possible:

> Samuel Spade's jaw was long and bony, his chin a jutting v under the more flexible v of his mouth. His nostrils curved back to make another, smaller v. His yellow-grey eyes were horizontal. The v motif was picked up again by thickish brows rising outward from the twin creases above a hooked nose, and his pale brown hair grew down—

from high flat temples—in a point on his forehead. He looked rather pleasantly like a blond satan.

— DASHIELL HAMMETT, THE MALTESE FALCON

Rather than a physical description, you could begin with a psychological profile instead:

Mack Bolan was not born to kill, as many of his comrades and superiors secretly believed. He was not a mechanically functioning killer-robot, as his snip-team partners openly proclaimed. He was not even a cold-blooded and ruthless exterminator, as one leftist news correspondent tagged him. Mack was simply a man who could command himself. He was the personification of the ideal advanced by the army psychologist who screened and evaluated sniper-team candidates: "A good sniper has to be a man who can kill methodically, unemotionally, and *personally. Personally* because it's an entirely different ball game when you can see even the color of your victim's eyes through the magnification of a sniper-scope, when you can see the look of surprise and fear when he realizes he's been shot. Most any good soldier can be a successful sniper *once*—it's the second or third time around, when the memories of personal killing are edged into the conscience, the the 'soldiers' are separated from the 'executioners.' Killing in this manner is closely akin to murder in the conscience of many men. Of course, we do not want mad dogs in this program, either. What we want, simply, is a man who can distinguish between murder and duty, and who can realize that a duty killing is not an act of murder. A man who is cool and calm when he himself is in jeopardy completes the picture of our sniper ideal."

Sergeant Mack Bolan was obviously such a man.

— DON PENDLETON, THE EXECUTIONER #1: WAR
AGAINST THE MAFIA

The author goes on to describe Bolan's official record of Vietnam kills (32), before delving into his personal life, leading up to the tragedy that claimed the lives of his family and set the hero on the path of revenge. Pendleton does this in a very matter-of-fact manner, using reports and personal correspondence. From there, he reveals Mack's initial revenge, setting the stage for Bolan to walk on fully-formed as "The Executioner."

The disadvantage to this approach is it can be construed as dispassionate, detached, even clinical. If that's the effect you want, great! But if it isn't, one solution is to inject a sense of mystery into an otherwise detached description of your heroes. By giving only certain facts and withholding others, you make this type of opening quite interesting.

> Almost everyone thought the man and boy were father and son.
>
> They crossed the country on a rambling southwest line in an old Citroen sedan, keeping mostly to secondary roads, traveling in fits and starts. They stopped in three places along the way before reaching their final destination: first in Rhode Island, where the tall man with the black hair worked in a textile mill; then in Youngstown, Ohio, where he worked three months on a tractor assembly line; and finally in a small California town near the Mexican border, where he pumped gas and worked at repairing small foreign cars with an amount of success that was, to him, surprising and gratifying.
>
> Wherever they stopped, he got a Maine newspaper called the Portland Press-herald and watched it for items concerning a small southern Maine town named Jerusalem's Lot and the surrounding area. There were such items from time to time.
>
> — STEPHEN KING, 'SALEM'S LOT

The hook here is subtle: "Almost everyone thought the man and boy were father and son." That tells us something is wrong. If it was a normal relationship, like uncle and nephew, the author would have told us. So the pair are unrelated. What are they doing together? Why are they crossing the country, sticking to back-roads? The mystery arises from the lack of information given.

Clearly, they are on the run, but from who? The law? The boy's family? Or something worse, something not of this world... something supernatural. An evil that claimed the town of 'Salem's Lot and almost claimed them as well. Perhaps that evil still hunts them even now.

Over the rest of this prologue, we get to know a little more about the man and boy: the man was a novelist "a million years ago" and is working on a new book, one he hopes to sell; the boy is haunted by nightmares. We learn they are linked by some great evil, and that the evil is not done.

Chapter one takes us back to the man's arrival in 'Salem's Lot, and we see how the evil began. What makes this work is that we know the genre (horror). We know it involves vampires taking over a small New England town. So we're willing to go along for the ride, certain Stephen King will pay our patience off down the road. Without a clear genre, readers might not be as willing.

Let's give the world's most popular genre a spin with this next example from romance queen Nora Roberts:

> By the time she was eight, Mackensie Elliot had been married fourteen times. She'd married each of her three best friends—as both bride and groom—her best friend's brother (under his protest), two dogs, three cats, and a rabbit.
>
> She'd served at countless other weddings as maid of honor, bridesmaid, groomsman, best man, and officiant.
>
> Though the dissolutions were invariably amicable, none of the the marriages had lasted an afternoon. The transitory aspect of marriage came as no surprise to Mac, as her own parents boasted two each —so far.
>
> — NORA ROBERTS, VISION IN WHITE

From this cute and clever opening, Roberts goes on a few more paragraphs about her hero's fascination with weddings, then reveals the one big moment in Mac's childhood that changed her life forever, taking what had been a fantasy and turning it into what would one day become her career: wedding photography.

On her eighth birthday, her father gives her an adult camera, and Mac goes from staging Barbie doll weddings to adult ones. Of course, this eventually leads to accidental romance, a romance Mac fights at first.

How will she fit this man in to her busy life? How can she make time for him and her business? Because the author has made Mac so charming right off the bat, readers will be turning pages to find out if this hero can turn yet another of her fantasies into reality with her own fairy tale wedding.

Now let's see how the hero describing himself sounds, and how it can be a more powerful way to hook readers than third person.

I am the vampire Lestat. I'm immortal, more or less. The light of the sun, the sustained heat of an intense fire—these things might destroy me. But then again, they might not.

— ANNE RICE, THE VAMPIRE LESTAT

First person infuses your story with a hint of memoir or autobiography. Done well, it can bring your hero to life in a way nothing else can. Anne Rice continues this trick throughout the sequels, and it serves as a convenient shorthand to bring new readers up to speed:

Lestat here. You know who I am? Then skip the next few paragraphs. For those whom I have not met before, I want this to be love at first sight.

Behold: your hero for the duration, a perfect imitation of a blond, blue-eyed, six-foot Anglo-Saxon male. A vampire, and one of the strongest you'll ever encounter.

— ANNE RICE, MEMNOCH THE DEVIL

Your hero doesn't have to undead to be interesting, in fact, they could even just be dead…

> My name was Salmon, like the fish; first name, Susie. I was fourteen when I was murdered on December 6, 1973. In newspaper photos of missing girls from the seventies, most looked like me: white girls with mousy brown hair. This was before kids of all races and genders started appearing on mil cartons or in the daily mail. It was still back when people believed things like that didn't happen.

> — ALICE SEBOLD, THE LOVELY BONES

We turn now to the hero's sidekick introducing the hero. Imagine the possibilities of Robin telling the story of Batman, and how different and fun that would be! What if the narrator wasn't the sidekick, but an employee or colleague of the hero, such as Commissioner Gordon or Alfred the butler?

What if it was the hero's love interest, such as Lois Lane telling the story of Superman? Mary Jane Watson or Gwen Stacy telling the story of Spider-Man?

Our heroes define us, and exploring alternate viewpoints like these can be just the thing to make your story stand out. Note that this approach also works for rivals, business partners, friends, students, children, siblings, or other family member. The trick is finding the best character to tell the hero's story. Ideally, that character should have agency of their own so they are not passive but instead take an active role in the story.

Finally, let's see how the villain narrating the hero's story might play out.

> Morgaine speaks…

> *In my time, I have been called many things: sister, lover, priestess, wise-woman, queen. Now in truth I have come to be wise-woman, and a time may come when these things may need to be known. But in sober truth, I think it is the Christians who will tell the last tale. For ever the world of Fairy drifts further from the world in which the Christ holds sway. I have no quarrel with*

the Christ, only with his priests, who call the Great Goddess a demon and deny that she ever held power in this world. At best, they say that her power was of Satan. Or else they clothe her in the blue robe of the Lady of Nazareth —who indeed had power in her way, too—and say that she was ever virgin. But what can a virgin know of the sorrows and travail of mankind?

And now, when the world has changed, and Arthur—my brother, my lover, king who was and king who shall be—lies dead (the common folk say sleeping) in the Holy Isle of Avalon, the tale should be told as it was before the priests of the White Christ came to cover it all with their saints and legends.

— MARION ZIMMER BRADLEY, THE MISTS OF AVALON

Bradley is going to tell us the story of Camelot—of King Arthur and the Knights of the Round Table—from the mouth of their enemy, the infamous witch, Morgaine Le Fay. Was Morgaine misunderstood and painted wrongly in the legends? Was she perhaps *the* hero, or at least *a* hero? What really happened? Admit it: you're intrigued.

STORY SECRET #3

VILLAINS AS HEROES

We live in difficult times. Complex times, where evil cloaks itself as good and good is branded evil. Deep down, most of us want to be good, even when we aren't. The weight of the world is just so much we don't know how to do it. But when our backs are against the wall, even the worst of us can have a moment of clarity and becomes heroes.

Villains as protagonists are growing in popularity, from the Wicked Witch in *The Wizard of Oz* taking center stage in *Wicked* to Walter White in *Breaking Bad*.

The trick is to make them likable and interesting, painting them as anti-heroes rather than villains. You do that by giving them relatable flaws and by pitting them against villains far more evil than they are. Stay tuned: I will speak more about about villains and their victims in Chapter 10.

4

MEETING

SOMETIMES CHANCE BRINGS two people together: chance, fate, or destiny. In most of the examples throughout this book, we meet one character at a time—either the hero or the villain. Sometimes other characters are present, but friend or foe, they are minor characters, supporting cast, and almost always previously known to the hero.

This chapter addresses what happens when two complete strangers meet and that becomes the hook. But they can't just be any characters. They must be the hero and hero, hero and sidekick, hero and love interest, hero and villain, hero and rival, hero and client, or any other major character who is going to play a major role in the story.

There's one more rule: *The meeting must occur in the first sentence.* If the characters do not meet there, then the meeting itself is not the hook and something else is.

I was going to call this chapter "Couples" but thought that too limiting. Not every meeting needs to be romantic or lead to romance. Meetings can lead to love, certainly, but they can also lead to fame, fortune, tragedy, adventure, any number of good or terrible things.

Cornell Woolrich, the greatest suspense writer of the twentieth century, handles his characters meeting like this:

Their eyes met in Rome. On a street in Rome—the Via Piemonte. He was coming down it, coming toward her, when she first saw him. She didn't know it but he was also coming into her life, into her destiny—bringing what was meant to be.

Every life is a mystery. And every story of every life is a mystery. But it is not what *happens* that is the mystery. It is whether it *has* to happen no matter what, whether it is ordered and ordained, fixed and fated, or whether it can be missed, avoided, circumvented, passed by; *that* is the mystery.

If she had not come along the Via Piemonte that day, would it still have happened? If she had come along the Via Piemonte that day, but ten minutes later than she did, would it *still* have happened? Therein lies the real mystery. And no one ever knows, and no one ever will.

As their eyes met, they held.

— CORNELL WOOLRICH, "FOR THE REST OF HER LIFE"

Woolrich begins with a couple meeting in the most beautiful, poetic terms possible ("Their eyes met in Rome"), then switches to mystery. This lets readers know this isn't going to be a love story in the normal sense. There's something deeper, something not quite right about the meeting. It has the added benefit of delaying reader gratification. Whenever possible, you want to keep readers guessing, wanting, craving answers, but not too long... just long enough. Knowing how long is too long is what separates a master of suspense from the novice.

Not all meetings begin favorably. In romance, the first encounter between the female hero and her lover almost always begins with them disliking each other. It is only later, through repeated actions, reactions, and misunderstandings, that they come to realize they love each other.

This initial dislike can also work outside romance, perhaps in the context of a "bromance" or professional rivalry. One of my favorite examples was turned into one of the most successful TV movies of all time, followed by a sequel and its own series, a line of novels, even a reboot TV series.

This is owed to the lovably obnoxious, irascible, and annoying character of Carl Kolchak (played to perfection by Darren McGavin). *A loser. A boozer.* But a hardboiled reporter who will do anything to get his story… and he will go into some very dark places to get it. Haunted places. Horror places. Even though he's scared as hell, Carl won't give up. In the end, that makes him even deadlier than the monsters he hunts.

> I first met Carl Kolchak in August of 1979 at a recording studio in Hollywood where my associate and I had been making some radio commercials for one of our larger accounts. Kolchak was there as a press representative for one of the actors we were using and I disliked him almost on sight. He was seedy, gross, aggressive, slightly drunk, and a general hindrance to all of us. But, he was also extremely persuasive in his later attempts to get me up to his shabby one-room apartment on the pretext of letting me in on "one of the biggest crime stories of the decade."
>
> — JEFF RICE, KOLCHAK: THE NIGHT STALKER

The crime story turns out to be a vampire stalking victims in Las Vegas… Nobody will believe him, and after driving a wooden stake through the vampire's heart, Carl is railroaded out of town by the mayor's office and law enforcement desperate to cover up the whole affair.

Thus in the sequel, Carl begins in a new town, working for a new paper, making his usual pain in the ass out of himself, when he stumbles on a new monster seeking victims. Again, nobody believes him. Again, Carl kills the monster, and again, he is run out of town for his efforts. The poor guy can't catch a break!

The author inserts himself into the story as the guy meeting Kolchak. This gimmick of Kolchak giving his "unpublishable" stories to Rice is repeated in the sequel, creating a frame device[1].

James M. Cain is most famous for *The Postman Always Rings Twice* and *Double Indemnity*. Both include ill-fated meetings in the first chapter, but it is his last novel that begins with one in the first sentence:

> I first met Tom Barclay at my husband's funeral, as he recalled to me later, though he made so little impression on me at the time that I had no recollection of ever having seen him before.
>
> — JAMES M. CAIN, THE COCKTAIL WAITRESS

Sure, Tom may not seem like much now, but he comes to play a major part in the story soon enough. Important enough the hero feels obligated to recall him now, in the first line of her tell-all confession of sex and murder. Without Tom, there might not be any need for her to tell anyone anything...

Note that *The Cocktail Waitress* uses the hero's recollection of a meeting she doesn't even remember. This shows that despite the restrictions of the meeting as a hook in the first sentence, you still have some wiggle room. Be creative!

Like romance, the *noir*, hardboiled, suspense, and crime genres seem perfect to begin with a meeting, particularly with a client. Here's an example:

> He stood in the doorway, staring at me and the office like a man who'd walked into the Christian Science Reading Room and found himself witnessing an appendectomy. He started to unbutton his topcoat, then changed his mind. He backed up a few steps and peered off down the hallway to to his right, as if there were something there that required his immediate attention. He looked up at the number above my office door. Then he stepped back into the room and blinked at me nervously.
>
> I don't get too many middle-aged people in my office. Maybe it's because they've heard I'm a hard-ass punk kid., which sometimes I am. Maybe they'd rather hire some retired traffic cop who'll drink martinis with them and make pleasant conversation. Or maybe they

only come to my office when I'm not around—which is most of the time.

"Something I can do for you?"

I try to be businesslike, despite the fact I don't like business and I don't like offices and I'd rather be warming a stool at Ralph's Bar instead of sitting behind a desk playing Nero Wolfe. But this guy smelled like money and the smell didn't hurt my nose too much. So I asked the question politely and he stared at me some more.

— BRAD LANG, CROCKETT ON THE LOOSE

With this example, the author tells us a lot about the two characters without ever using their names. Of course, that comes next when the uptight middle-aged client hires "young, hip, long-haired" private detective Freddy Crockett to find his wayward teenage daughter.

The characters' initial meeting doesn't have to be romantic, or even poetic. It can simply be humorous.

I was fifteen years old when I first met Sherlock Holmes, fifteen years old with my nose in a book as I walked the Sussex Downs, and nearly stepped on him.

— LAURIE R. KING, THE BEEKEEPER'S APPRENTICE

This hook is funny on multiple levels, and adds a bit of action besides. We immediately get a sense of who the hero is, and because Sherlock Holmes is the world's most famous detective, the author doesn't need to waste words describing him. We know who he is, and because of that, we have a good idea what kind of story this will be.

STORY SECRET #4

INSERT YOURSELF (OR SOMEONE FAMOUS)

Remember when I was talking about author Jeff Rice inserting himself into his Kolchak novels? This is a cute gag. It also makes the book very "meta," which is a hip way to say it blurs the line between fiction and reality. What that does is make the story feel more real, especially if *maybe* it could happen in real life. Hey, we don't know there's no such thing as vampires, we only think they don't exist—which is exactly the way the vampires want it!

But seriously, this could be a fun running gag. It can also be a way for you to get into the story and really get to know your hero. Yeah, Kolchak's a crazy old bastard, and sure, he's kind of a terrible person, but he's also a guy who gets things done, and you gotta respect that. Behind the gruff exterior, he's also a bit of a softie, and loyal to his friends, in his own messed-up way. What is your hero like? If your answer is "perfect," do not pass go. Do not collect $200.

Give your hero flaws. Give yourself flaws, because guess what? You have them. We all do. And when you're a character in a book, they get magnified. And maybe they even get worked on, even fixed.

But Jackson, you say, I can't put myself in my story! Nobody wants to read about me. Depends on how interesting you make yourself, but OK, sure... You invent all these crazy characters for your story, but you can't re-invent yourself on the page? Come on, you're a writer! At least that's what you told me when you bought this book.

Maybe you've got a point though. I'm listening. Maybe what you need is to replace yourself with someone who has more *star power*. Well, look no farther than your nearest public domain characters. Can you find a way to introduce Sherlock Holmes, Great Cthulhu, Mr. D'Arcy, or the Wizard of Oz into your story? What about some famous dead guy like Edgar Allan Poe, Aristotle, or George Washington? Plenty of other authors have pulled this off, sometimes even letting the dead celebrity take center stage as the hero. There's a ton of fun books like that out: *Pride & Prejudice & Zombies*, *Sense & Sensibility & Sea Monsters*, *Abraham Lincoln, Vampire Hunter*, etc.

CHAPTER 4 FOOTNOTES

- 1 See Chapter 16: Prologue or Frame.

MONOLOGUE

WHILE DIFFERENT DEFINITIONS of monologue exist, for the purpose of this book I mean a literary device by which the reader gains access to the interior thoughts and emotions of a character. This is usually called "internal monologue," but I'll shorten it here to just monologue.

Monologue has several advantages over dialogue, chiefly its intimacy. We are firmly rooted in the head of your hero. The second advantage is it operates in the realm of thought, not speech, and theoretically, that frees you to talk about anything. But whatever is thought or said must be filtered through the viewpoint of the hero, so it may not be entirely factual.

This is especially true in the case of unreliable narrators who may lie to the reader, omit important facts, or steadfastly believe certain untruths, such as Holden Caulfield in J.D. Salinger's *The Catcher in the Rye.*

The disadvantages to monologue are the same as its strengths. Your hero must be instantly likable. That doesn't mean perfect. That means flawed, but with strong potential.

In the case of anti-heroes, they must be interesting, if not likable, though it's better if they have some good qualities too—even if it's just a code of honor. Something that separates your anti-hero from the villains he must fight and makes him look good by comparison.

This isn't always possible, however, so be sure your irredeemably broken anti-heroes are fascinating in some way that gives readers a reason to stick with them. Jeff Lindsay's *Dexter* series immediately comes to mind, as do the twisted anti-heroes of crime writer Jim Thompson:

> I'd gotten out of my car and was running for the porch when I saw her. She was peering through the curtains of the door, and a flash of lightning lit up the dark glass for an instant, framing her face like a picture. And it wasn't a pretty picture, by any means; she was about as far from a raving beauty as I was. But something about it kind of got me. I tripped over a crack, and almost went sprawling. When I looked up again she was gone, and the curtains were closed.
>
> — JIM THOMPSON, A HELL OF A WOMAN

As we've seen with action and dialogue, *in media res* is often the best way to go. In this example, we don't need to hear the narrator tell us about how he woke up and ate breakfast. Always begin as close to the moment your hero's life changes as possible.

Jim Thompson, best known for *The Getaway*, *The Grifters*, and *The Killer Inside Me*, has a perfect monologue to hook readers in *A Hell of a Woman*. He paints the scene vividly, introducing his twisted hero and love interest at the exact moment they first lay eyes on each other, which he wisely works into the first sentence.

This is a dark story of bubbling madness and murder, so it's only fitting that Thompson treats it almost like a horror movie, with the flash of lightning serving as both a warning and a reveal. The self-deprecating way the hero refers to his and her lack of beauty is a hint these characters may be far uglier inside than out.

Still, the hero recognizes something in her that moves him. The hero tripping is a warning to him to turn back, just like the lightning was. When he ignores it and sees she's gone, he is given a third chance to turn back. Naturally, he ignores that too:

> I limped on up the steps, set my sample case down and rang the bell. I stepped back from the door and waited, working up a big smile, taking a gander around the yard.

The limp is the pay-off for the fall. It helps humanize the hero. The sample case and him "working up a big smile" tell us he must be a traveling salesman. Notice Thompson doesn't have anyone answer the door yet. He's delaying reader gratification to fill us in on the setting:

> It was a big old-fashioned dwelling, a half-mile or so beyond the state university campus and the only house in that block. Judging by its appearance and location, I guessed that it had probably been a farmhouse at one time.

The fact that it is the only house on the block and removed from the prosperity of the university is subtle symbolism for the loneliness, isolation, and failure of the hero and love interest. It's also another warning for the hero to stay away.

> I punched the bell again. I held my finger on it, listening to its dimly shrill clatter inside the house. I pulled the screen open and began pounding on the door. You did things like that when you worked for Pay-E-Zee Stores. You got used to people who hid when they saw you coming.

Here we get the name of the hero's employer and the fact that he doesn't take no for an answer. He knows the woman is in there and we get the feeling he's more desperate to make a human connection than a sale.

> The door flew open while I was still beating on it. I took one look at this dame and moved back fast. It wasn't the young one, the haunted-

looking babe I'd seen peering through the curtains. This was an old biddy with a beak like a hawk and close-set, mean little eyes. She was about seventy—I don't know how anyone could have got that ugly in less than seventy years—but she looked hale and hearty. She was carrying a heavy cane, and I got the impression that she was ready to use it. On me.

Instead of giving us the romantic encounter we expect, Thompson confronts our determined hero with an equally determined obstacle: a cruel gatekeeper who stands in his way.

This is delaying reader satisfaction at its finest! We know the "haunted-looking babe" is inside, maybe even listening just out of sight, and the hero will have to do some fast-talking to get by the old woman and meet her. The old woman is also the final warning the hero should turn back.

Your opening monologue doesn't have to be that long. Let's take a look at a similar doomed love story to see how quickly that author transitions out of monologue:

> She wasn't what you would call beautiful. She was just a red-haired girl with a lot of sock. She stood behind the screen door on the front porch, frowning at me.
>
> "I'm Jack Ruxton," I said. "From Ruxton's TV. Sorry I'm late."
>
> — GIL BREWER, THE VENGEFUL VIRGIN

See how it's the same thing, only shorter? There's a reason this story doesn't delay Jack and his love interest from meeting. Unlike our haunted friend from *A Hell of a Woman*, the girl in *The Vengeful Virgin* is the guardian of the other occupant in the house:

> She was maybe seventeen or eighteen. The porch light was on. It was about eight o'clock on a Monday night. Looking past her, I could see through a long, broad living room, expensively furnished, and on into a brightly lighted bedroom. A man with iron-gray hair lay on a

hospital bed under a sheet, with his toes sticking straight up. His head was flung back as if he were in a cramp. There was a lot of tricky-looking paraphernalia, rubber hoses and tanks and stuff, beside the bed. A fluorescent bed light glared across his face. It was eerie.[1]

"Well," I said. "TV on the blink?"

"No. That's not what I called you for, Mr. Ruxton."

Maybe you've caught on that Shirley is not just the guardian of the old man, but also a *femme fatale* luring the hero into her web of murder for profit. And speaking of bad girls, no one writes them better than Megan Abbott:

I want the legs.

That was the first thing that came into my head. The legs of a twenty-year-old Vegas showgirl, a hundred feet long and with just enough curve and give and promise. Sure, there was no hiding the slightly worn hands or the beginning tugs of skin framing the bones in her face. But the legs, they lasted, I tell you. They endured. Two decades her junior, my skinny matchsticks were no competition.

In the casinos, she could pass for thirty. The low lighting, her glossy auburn hair, legs swinging, tapping the bottom rim of the tall bettor stools. At the track, though, she looked her age. Even swathed in oversized sunglasses, a wide-brimmed hat, bright gloves, she couldn't outflank the merciless sunshine, the glare off the grandstand. Not that it mattered. She was legend.

I was never sure what she saw in me. *You looked like you knew a thing or two,* she told me later. *But you were ready to learn a lot more.*

— MEGAN ABBOTT, QUEENPIN

From the mysterious first line, "I want the legs," to the tantalizing, "I knew you were ready to learn a lot more," Abbott knows how to hook you, seducing readers as easily as her hero with the promise of fast times and easy money.

Did you notice the one thing *A Swell-Looking Babe, The Vengeful*

Virgin, and *Queenpin* all have in common? They prove opening with your hero observing or remembering another person is a powerful way to begin. You can pull off a similar effect using an event or place instead of a person.

STORY SECRET #5

MONOLOGUE MAKES IT "REAL"

By getting inside your hero's head and staying there, monologue doesn't distance the reader. That's because it makes fiction read like memoir, blurring the lines between what is real and what isn't, and that can be very appealing.

Don't miss the *special nonfiction bonus section* on writing dynamite story hooks for memoir in Part III; they all use compelling monologue to hook readers. The memoir examples absolutely apply to fiction writers too, so if you want more monologue examples, be sure to read them.

Examples include everyone from soldiers to junkies to rock stars —they all have something interesting to say.

CHAPTER 5 FOOTNOTES

- 1 This is a prime example of telling, not showing. "It was eerie" adds nothing to the reader's understanding that the creepy crippled guy on the bed didn't already provide.

MYSTERY

A MYSTERY MUST INTRIGUE the reader, raising a question worth answering. It is often expressed in the form of dialogue or monologue, though there is no hard or fast rule. Nor must mystery be phrased as a question, as Ayn Rand famously begins *Atlas Shrugged*:

"Who is John Galt?"

The light was ebbing, and Eddie Willers could not distinguish the bum's face. The bum had said it simply, without expression. But from the sunset far at the end of the street, yellow glints caught in his eyes, and the eyes looked straight at Eddie Willers, mocking and still—as if the question had been addressed to the causeless uneasiness within him.

"Why did you say that?" asked Eddie Willers, his voice tense.

The bum leaned against the side of the doorway; a wedge of broken glass behind him reflected the metal yellow of the sky.[1]

"Why does it bother you?" he asked.

"It doesn't," snapped Eddie Willers.

— AYN RAND, ATLAS SHRUGGED

But clearly, it does trouble Eddie. In fact, this question becomes the book's theme and most repeated line. While John Galt does exist, he has vanished, and his disappearance becomes a metaphor for why the world is falling apart.

Galt represents innovation, passion, and rewards for superior thinking. Without him, and men and women like him, we are left with backward, unmotivated fools in charge of society. Fools who think they are "helping" people by rewarding mediocrity. When everyone gets an award, nothing is worth winning.

Atlas Shrugged is the quest not just to find and restore the actual John Galt, but to find and restore the John Galt within each of us. It takes over a thousand pages and three movies to do it, but eventually the mystery is solved.

But what if one mystery is not enough? And what if you don't want to spend a thousand pages exploring them? Let's see how this next story handles it:

Outside the blood spirals down.

> — DAN SIMMONS, "SHAVE AND A HAIRCUT, TWO
> BITES"

We think we know what the author means, and the mystery that immediately comes to mind is, "Who died and how?" But as the next paragraph reveals, we don't know anything yet:

I pause at the entrance to the barbershop. There is nothing unique about it. Almost certainly there is one similar to it in your community; it's function is proclaimed by the pole outside, the red spiraling down, and by the name painted on the broad window, the letters grown scabrous as the gold paint ages and flakes away. While the most expensive hair salons now bear the names of their owners, and the shopping mall franchises offer sickening cutenesses— Hairport, Hair Today: Gone Tomorrow, Hair We Are, Headlines, Shear Masters, The Head Hunter, In-Hair-itance, and so forth, ad nauseum—the name of this shop is eminently forgettable. It is meant to be so. This shop offers neither styling nor unisex cuts. If your hair is dirty when you enter, it will be cut dirty; there are no shampoos given here. While the franchises demand $15 to $30 for a basic haircut, the cost here has not changed for a decade or more. It occurs to the potential new customer immediately upon entering that no one could live on an income based upon such low rates. No one does. The potential customer usually beats a hasty retreat, put off by the too-low prices, by the darkness of the place, by the air of dusty decrepitude exuded from both the establishment itself and from its few waiting customers, invariably silent and staring, and by the strange sense of tension bordering upon threat which hangs in the stale air.

Ha! We thought someone had died, then we learn the "blood" spiral is merely a barbershop pole. No one's dead. Mystery solved, right? That one, yes, but Dan Simmons immediately sets up another (by combining mystery and setting). The second is far more troubling than the first—and more relatable. Few of us have ever seen a dead body outside a horror movie, but everyone has stumbled across a dusty, disused shop and wondered how the hell it stays open.

We immediately conjure up all kinds of hellish ideas— *Sweeney Todd, the Demon Barber of Fleet Street* being most likely. Slit throats instead of close shaves. Bodies ground to burgers and sold at the butcher shop next door. That sort of thing. Now it's not just the idea of one person dying outside, but the hint a lot of people may have died inside this shop. And from the title, the idea of a vampire barber shop is just too delicious to ignore.

Mysteries can take many forms, so let's examine as many mysterious first lines as we can:

It all started with X-Ray Specs.

— NANCY A. COLLINS, "APHRA"

This is great! X-ray glasses are a child's toy, a famous rip-off from the golden age of mail order. What could they possibly do to set off an exciting chain of events?

> It is true that I have sent six bullets through the head of my best friend, and yet I hope to show by this statement that I am not his murderer.
>
> — H.P. LOVECRAFT, "THE THING ON THE DOORSTEP"

Classic Lovecraft! Either the narrator is insane or about to tell a truth so terrible, everyone will believe he is.

> I lost an arm on my last trip home.
>
> — OCTAVIA E. BUTLER, KINDRED

A great hook, as fascinating as it is frightening. This matter-of-fact recollection of human mutilation instantly disturbs the reader and guarantees they have to read more.

> Someone was murdering the small animals of our neighborhood.
>
> — CHRIS ADRIAN, "STAB"

Yikes! This lets you know right away a psycho is on the loose, and worse, that said psycho is one of the neighbors!

> I woke up wearing someone else's smile.
>
> — MICK GARRIS, "CHOCOLATE"

One of the best opening lines I've read. Is this the result of a *Freaky Friday* body swap, demonic possession, or plastic surgery?

I know I should call the police about William.

— R.L. STINE, "THE SPELL"

Reader sympathy and trust is established in one line. We instantly want the narrator to call the police on William before we even know who he is or what he's done.

The scream was distant and brief.

— DEAN KOONTZ, PHANTOMS

This kind of opening is good if you want to establish an air of danger or mystery without immediately putting your hero in jeopardy.

Heidi Williams sat on the hard, wooden bench of the Fairfield Police Station.

— CHRISTOPHER GREYSON, GIRL JACKED

Here we get the character's name and location, but it's the bench that's the star. Its description ("hard, wooden") alludes to unbending justice, or perhaps to corrupt law enforcement. Is Heidi a criminal or victim? Or maybe she's there to bail someone out. See how this one line gets us thinking?

Let's examine a few first paragraphs to see how different authors build on their mysterious opening lines:

They found me in the gutter. The night was the only thing I had left and not much of it at that. I heard the car stop, the doors open and shut and two voices talking. A pair of arms jerked me to my feet and held me there.

— MICKEY SPILLANE, THE GIRL HUNTERS

A grabber! Is the narrator drunk, insane, beat up, or dying? It turns out he's drunk, and has been for seven years, ever since his girlfriend died. He feels responsible, and has tried to destroy himself the only way he knows how to make up for it.

Of course, shortly after being picked up by the cops, he gets a clue his girlfriend isn't dead after all, which immediately motivates him to sober up. This isn't going to be some depressing *Leaving Las Vegas* sob story, but a hardboiled Mike Hammer crime novel. Yeah, baby!

> He was the ghastliest hitchhiker who ever thumbed me. He rose on his knees in the ditch. His eyes were black holes in his yellow face, his mouth a bright smear of red like a clown's painted grin. The arm he raised overbalanced him. He fell forward on his face again.
>
> — ROSS MCDONALD, FIND A VICTIM

Who is the ghastly hitchhiker and who hurt him? You can bet the hero is going to find out!

STORY SECRET #6

HOW TO START A SERIES IN ANY GENRE

While researching this book, I noticed that bestselling mystery[2] authors rarely seem to open their stories with mystery.[3] Instead, they provide details about their hero's past or present *before* the mystery enters the picture.[4] This is almost always done through monologue.

After seeing this pattern emerge time and time again, I decided to see how authors in other genres opened their series. Unfortunately, I found they tended to follow the same pattern. Why unfortunately? Because all too often these opening details are boring or irrelevant to the upcoming case. The standard introduction runs a few paragraphs to maybe a page or two, sometimes even a whole chapter, but the length doesn't matter. Boring is boring.

On the other hand, these "classic" openings are a hallmark of the mystery genre, and series in general. To give readers both what they expect *and* avoid the problem of putting them to sleep, my best advice is to combine the classic hero introduction with one of the ten ways I suggest, but to do so in an expedited fashion. Get in and out in a paragraph if you can (see Story Secret #5), and make sure your first sentence sings![5]

I know you'll want to see an example of the "classic way" to contrast with the kind of series opening I'm advocating. With all due respect, I'm going to reach back in time to perhaps the most famous mystery series of all. To me, this is the one that sets the boring opening precedent:

> In the year 1878, I took my degree of Doctor of Medicine of the University of London, and proceeded to Netley to go through the course prescribed for surgeons in the army. Having completed my studies there, I was duly attached to the Fifth Northumberland Fusiliers as Assistant Surgeon. The regiment was stationed in India at the time and before I could join it, the second Afghan war had broken out. On landing in Bombay, I learned that my corps had advanced through the passes, and was already deep in the enemy's country. I followed, however, with many other officers who were in the same situation as myself, and succeeded in reaching Kandahar in safety, where I found my regiment, and at once entered my new duties.
>
> — SIR ARTHUR CONAN DOYLE, "A STUDY IN SCARLET"

There's no hook! Worse, this is nothing but an info-dump[6] for Dr. Watson's backstory. And it goes on about his Afghan tour for *two more paragraphs*, then rambles on to him coming back to London, meeting a guy named Stamford at a bar, and only *then* finding out about Sherlock Holmes! It's interminable. Surely there must be a payoff for all this, right? Let's jump ahead to Holmes' and Watson's first meeting to see what kind of reward Doyle gives us:

> "Dr. Watson, Mr. Sherlock Holmes," said Stamford, introducing us.[7]

"How are you?" he said cordially, gripping my hand with a strength for which I should hardly have given him credit. "You have been in Afghanistan, I perceive."

"How on earth did you know that?" I asked in amazement.[8]

"Never mind," said he, chuckling to himself. "The question now is about hemoglobin. No doubt you see the significance of this discovery of mine?"

Seriously? Doyle's only reason for bogging down his opening with an info-dump is to set up how clever Holmes is? This is not a good payoff for such a longwinded opening! If Doyle was going to go to all the trouble to set this up, he should have explained *how* Holmes knew Watson had recently been in Afghanistan—otherwise, the reader is likely to feel cheated and angry. I know I did.

In my opinion, it would have been far better to open with Watson at the bar. Details of his past could have been slipped in there. For example, if I were writing this story, I might change the opening to:

Have you ever seen a man die? I have. Rooms of them. It's not like the stories they tell of noble heroes falling in battle. I'm sure a few go that way, but none of the ones I've seen. I'm talking about slow death in hospital tents. Where sometimes it's better to die whole than come out half a man. I saved as many as I could, however I could, even when they begged me to let them die.

Now I was done, the second Afghan War behind me. I was back in London, but not ready to go home. There were still demons that needed purging, but I'd had no luck with that, so I thought I'd drown them instead. The Criterion Bar seemed as good a place as any.

I was on my third round when someone tapped me on the shoulder. I turned to see my old buddy, Stamford, who I hadn't seen since before the war. I invited him to sit down and help me forget.

This gets right to the point. You feel the horror of war and the toll it takes. You get a far better sense of who Watson is without overwhelming the reader with too many details. No one cares where

Watson went to school, what army division he was attached to, or any of that travelogue stuff. It has zero impact on the reader and zero relevance to the story. Now, I'm not claiming my version is perfect[9], but it speeds the story along and does more to humanize Watson in one paragraph than Doyle does in three. That's because I'm *showing* how Watson's backstory emotionally impacts the present. We see a talented but flawed man in need of change, but without any idea how to get there—the "perfect" imperfect hero.

I'll end this chapter with one last bit of series advice: If you must recap events from previous book(s), do so as briefly as you can. *But only if it's required for the new story to make sense!* See the chapter on prologues for more ideas on how to do this.

~

CHAPTER 6 FOOTNOTES

- 1 The bum, broken glass, doorway, and sunset are symbolism for a shattered society at death's door, as is "metal yellow" for gold (money). This suggests only through economic recovery via bold innovation and rewarding excellence can humanity be lifted to new heights.
- 2 By "mystery," I mean a story featuring a crime-solving hero who actively pursues an unknown villain in order to right a wrong. Thrillers, on the other hand, feature the hero being actively pursued by a known villain (for whatever reason: revenge, eliminating the hero as a witness, etc.).
- 3 The sole exception is some show a murder or other plot-related crime committed in a prologue.
- 4 This is also frequently true of fiction series featuring a recurring hero, regardless of genre.
- 5 Look to the examples from Mickey Spillane's "Mike Hammer" and Ross McDonald's "Lew Archer" series in

Chapter 1. These both show easy, exciting ways to avoid a boring series opening!

- <u>6</u> For more about the dreaded info-dump and why it's the kiss of death, see Chapter 17: Telling or Info-Dumping.
- <u>7</u> This is redundant writing that simply tells us what the dialogue has already shown.
- <u>8</u> Doyle is once again telling us what his dialogue has just shown.
- <u>9</u> No doubt Doyle fans will agree.

PREMONITION

PREMONITION IS an overwhelming but unprovable feeling that something important is about to happen. Usually, it's the anticipation of a negative event, but can be felt prior to positive events as well.

> Twenty minutes before the quake hit, Stanley Banks was standing at his living room window.
>
> — RICHARD LAYMON, QUAKE

From the first sentence, we know the catalyst—indeed, the very title of the book—is only scant pages away, a few chapters at most. We know Stanley is in danger, but poor Stanley doesn't. We fear for him, wonder who he is, and what we would do if we were in a similar situation.

That's the power of premonition: wondering what you might do if you knew you something awful was about to happen. The premonition is a subtle but powerful spur to the reader's imagination. It makes them read on, not only to find out what happens to Stanley, but to see if they would make the same decisions he does if they were in a similar situation (and if you've read *Quake*, hopefully you won't!).

Premonition is a two-part opening that is always combined with another of the ten ways every story should begin—often action or mystery. That's because you can't give away the surprise without setting up a mystery to go with it. That would be like serving a cake with no frosting!

In the case of the above example, the mystery is related to Stanley's survival after the quake than what he's doing beforehand. That's because Stanley has no control over the quake. Even knowing about it, or having a premonition it was coming wouldn't prevent the quake from happening.

You might think a guy standing at his living room window is weak for an opening, and ordinarily, you'd be right, but what Richard Laymon is hiding from you in that first sentence is that what Stanley's doing at the window actually plays a huge role in the horror that happens after the quake, and if the quake had never happened, then the horror might not have either.

Maybe you prefer a more subtle form of fear than leading with an earthquake. If that's the case, you might consider the "slow burn." Although the following opening line *appears* neutral and is not itself a premonition, the two lines that follow (paired with the sinister title) are what make the paragraph a premonition and give it its punch:

I was eleven. That's probably the reason for it. You don't know or understand *yourself* when you're eleven.

Daddy had been gone two years and Mom had just been fired from the grocery. She took a job as a cocktail waitress. At the time I thought the name had something to do with the skirt that showed off her legs clear up to here. That's the trouble with being eleven. You know there are secret things you are supposed to understand but no one has taken the trouble to explain them to you yet so sometimes you see something and the world flips completely over and you think, Oh, *that's* what she meant when she—

But anyway, I was eleven and mostly I was alone at night. People think too much when they're alone. Mom does it. She sits and drinks and thinks. Of course, I'm there but to Mom that's the same as being alone. She thinks about something I did or something Daddy did and how much I'm like him and pretty soon it gets all mixed up in her head and she hits me. So I know how dangerous it is to be alone and thinking.

— JULEEN BRANTINGHAM, "HOLLY, DON'T TELL"

And Brantingham keeps going, building the mystery, the mounting dread *something terrible* is going to happen!

Let's see how America's favorite storyteller, Louis L'Amour, handles the "slow burn" in his beloved western, *Hondo*:

He rolled a cigarette in his lips, liking the taste of the tobacco, squinting his eyes against the sun glare. His buckskin shirt, seasoned by sun, rain, and sweat, smelled stale and old. His jeans had long since faded to a neutral color that lost itself against the desert.

He was a big man, wide-shouldered, with the lean, hard-boned face of the desert rider. There was no softness in him. His toughness was ingrained and deep, without cruelty, yet quick, hard, and dangerous. Whatever wells of gentleness might lie within him were guarded and deep.

An hour passed and there was no more dust, so he knew he was in trouble. He had drawn up short of the crest where his eyes could see over the ridge, his horse crowded against a dark clump of juniper where he was invisible to any eye not in the immediate vicinity.

The day was still and hot. Sweat trickled down his cheeks and down his body under his shirt. Dust meant a dust devil or riders... and this had been no dust devil.

— LOUIS L'AMOUR, HONDO

L'Amour creates the slow burn by building up his hero first, only gradually revealing the sense of uneasiness dwelling within him. Riders are after him, but who? Bandits? Apaches? Or is it the law? We don't know, but like any master of the craft, L'Amour won't keep us waiting long; his hero is attacked by the end of the page three.

Back to the direct approach. In the event of villains acting against your hero, there are a lot more variables:

The night Vincent was shot he saw it coming. The guy approached out of the streetlight on the corner of Meridian and Sixteenth, South Beach, and he reach-ed Vincent as he was walking from his car to his apartment building. It was early, a few minutes past nine.

Vincent turned his head to look at the guy and there was a moment when he could have taken him and did consider it, hit the guy as hard as he could. But Vincent was carrying a sack of groceries. He wasn't going to drop a half-gallon of Gallo Hearty Burgundy, a bottle of prune juice, and a jar of Ragu spaghetti sauce on the sidewalk. Not even when the guy showed his gun, called him a motherfucker through his teeth and said he wanted Vincent's wallet and all the money he had on him.

— ELMORE LEONARD, GLITZ

There are sexy ways to open with premonition too:

Petra's letters should have warned me. Those secret, smiling letters written in an overbold hand with violet ink on pale green perfumed paper, sealed in green envelopes. They should have been warning enough for anyone. And the house should have warned me. The minute I stepped through the doorway at 13 French Street, I sensed something was wrong—something I couldn't nail down. But she closed the door before I had a chance to run. So, you see, it was already too late. Only I should have run anyway…

— GIL BREWER, 13 FRENCH STREET

What sinister secret is Petra holding back from the hero? It's pretty obvious she wants to seduce him, but why? What is their relationship?

Who else is involved? You can bet *13 French Street* is going to be a real *noir* scorcher!

Money can be a good way to open with premonition:

> It started out as kind of a joke, but then it wasn't funny anymore because money became involved.
>
> — CHARLES WILLEFORD, THE SHARK-INFESTED CUSTARD

This kind of opening is disturbing but fun. The reader knows something's up, but can't quite put his finger on it.

Too much happiness or good luck can also be used as a springboard to disaster:

> It had been a pretty good day in many ways, so I might have known it would turn out bad.
>
> — JIM THOMPSON, THE CRIMINAL

As we've seen before, Jim Thompson always knows how to start things right. Let's see how a famous Young Adult fiction novel handles its opening premonition:

> Yesterday, I remember thinking I was the happiest person in the whole earth, in all of God's creation.
>
> — ANONYMOUS, GO ASK ALICE

You just know things are going bad, right? It's so easily set up. The past tense "I remember thinking" is what does it, along with its "yesterday" preface. These immediately clue you in to the fact the hero is in trouble and that her trouble is recent.

Here's another Young Adult classic, and this sets up the premonition so subtly, so simply, it's perfect:

The note was there, lying beside her plate when she came down to breakfast.

> — LOIS DUNCAN, I KNOW WHAT YOU DID LAST
> SUMMER

The title and knowing it's a horror/thriller tells you whatever that note contains, it's going to be bad news for the hero!

Let's close out this chapter with another dead simple premonition:

It was a perfect day for a drive.

> — RICHARD CHRISTIAN MATHESON, "DEAD END"

Again, the genre lets you know "the perfect day" is going to end in disaster. If this were a romance novel, you'd have entirely different expectations from seeing the words "It was a perfect day..."

These opening premonitions establish the heroes in their happy, Ordinary World, then promise to shatter it all in one sentence. Like the other examples in this chapter, they don't do it immediately, but rather delay reader gratification until the last possible moment.

STORY SECRET #7

GET IN AND GET OUT

Rather than be tied to this chapter, this story secret is universal. It not only works for *any* opening, it should be applied to every scene in your entire story.

There's a delicate balance between opening your story too fast and opening too slow. No hard and fast rules exist in fiction, as you can see from the wildly different examples in this book. Yet they all have something in common: *they only take as much time as they need to get in and get out.* If you're telling an action story, then you need to move faster. If you're telling a moody mystery or horror story, you can take a little more time. Not a lot more, but a little. Never bore your reader.

PROFOUND STATEMENT

PERHAPS THE TRICKIEST WAY to begin is with a profound statement:

The secret is how to die.

— DAN BROWN, THE LOST SYMBOL

Some authors offer only a single line like Dan Brown, or a few explanatory sentences before switching to how it relates to the hero:

Some people are just born evil. No twisted childhood trauma, no abusive stepfather, or alcoholic mother, just plain God-awful mean. Dr. Jasmine Cooper, dream therapist and empath, believed that, knew that. She had spent too many years looking inside the minds of murderers not to believe it.

— LAURELL K. HAMILTON, "HERE BE DRAGONS"

This is about as fast as you can get in and get out. How much time you devote to your statement is a matter of personal preference and the needs of your story. The more you expand your profound statement, the more atmosphere and meaning you can inject:

> The dead have highways. They run, unerring lines of ghost-trains, of dream-carriages, across the wasteland behind our lives, bearing an endless traffic of deported souls. Their thrum and throb can be heard in the broken places of the world, through cracks made by acts of cruelty, violence and depravity. Their freight, the wandering dead, can be glimpsed when the heart is close to bursting, and sights that should be hidden come plainly into view.
>
> They have sign-posts, these highways, and bridges and laybys. They have turn-pikes and intersections.
>
> It is at these intersections, where the crowds of dead mingle and cross, that this forbidden highway is most likely to spill through into our world. The traffic is heavy at the cross-roads, and the voices of the dead are at their most shrill. Here the barriers that separate one reality from the next are worn thin with the passage of innumerable feet.
>
> Such an intersection on the highway of the dead was located at Number 65, Tollington Place. Just a brick-fronted, mock-Georgian detached house, Number 65 was unremarkable in every other way. An old, forgettable house, stripped of the cheap grandeur it had once lain claim to, it had stood empty for a decade or more.
>
> — CLIVE BARKER, "THE BOOK OF BLOOD"

Barker gently eases you into his ghostly horror, each paragraph building on the one before it, culminating in the set up to his haunted house, which ties his statement into his story. Regardless of length, all profound statements must tie into your story.

Here's another example of a long statement, this time from Barker's comrade-in-fright, Stephen King:

> The most important things are the hardest things to say. They are the things you get ashamed of, because words diminish them—words shrink things that seemed limitless when they were in your head to no

more than living size when they're brought out. But it's more than that, isn't it? The most important things lie too close to wherever your secret heart is buried, like landmarks to a treasure your enemies would love to steal away. And you may make revelations that cost you dearly only to have people look at you in a funny way, not understanding what you've said at all, or why you thought it was so important that you almost cried while you were saying it. That's the worst, I think. When the secret stays locked within not for want of a teller but for want of an understanding ear.

I was twelve going on thirteen when I saw a dead human being. It happened in 1960, a long time ago... although sometimes it doesn't seem that long to me. Especially on the nights I wake up from dreams where the hail falls into his open eyes.

— STEPHEN KING, "THE BODY"

Like Barker, King eases you into the horror, telling you things any reader can identify with right up until he reveals the dead body. Sneaky, huh? Now it's too late to turn back. You're hooked! Also notice how he combines his profound statement with monologue for maximum effect.

Let's see how another great author handles combining the two:

I've got a story to tell, like everybody else in the world. Because that's what makes up life, isn't? Sure. Everybody's got a story—about somebody they met, or something that's happened to them, something they've done, something they want to do, something they'll never do. In the life of everybody on this old spinning ball there's a story about a road not taken, or a love that went bad, or a ghost of some kind. You know what I mean. You've got one too.

Well, I want to tell you a story. Trouble is, there are so *many* things I remember about Greystone Bay. I could tell you about what Joey Hammers and I found in the wreck of an old Chevy down where the blind man lives amid the junked cars. I could tell you about the time snakes started coming out of old lady Farrow's faucets, and what she did with them. I could tell you about the Elvis Presley impersonator who came to town, and went crazy when he couldn't get his makeup off. Oh yeah, I know a lot about what goes in Greystone Bay. Some things I wouldn't want to tell you after the sun goes down, but I want to tell you a story about *me*. You decide if it's a story worth telling.

— ROBERT R. MCCAMMON, "THE RED HOUSE"

McCammon uses a different tactic than Barker or King, opting for a more casual approach while teasing the reader with his hero's different memories (notice how each adds to the mystery and horror), before deciding on the memory this story will be about.

Why does he do that? Because if those other weird events weren't important enough to tell, then the one the hero has settled on must be even scarier!

Let's move on from the masters of horror to a master of crime and dirty politics:

America was never innocent. We popped our cherry on the boat over and looked back with no regrets. You can't ascribe our fall from grace to any single event or set of circumstances. You can't lose what you lacked at conception.

Mass-market nostalgia gets you hopped up for a past that never existed. Hagiography[1] sanctifies shuck-and-jive politicians and reinvents their expedient gestures as moments of great moral weight. Our continuing narrative line is blurred past truth and hindsight. Only a reckless verisimilitude can set that line straight.

The real Trinity of Camelot was Look Good, Kick Ass, Get Laid. Jack Kennedy was the mythological front man for a particularly juicy slice of our history. He talked a slick line and wore a world-class haircut. He was Bill Clinton minus pervasive media scrutiny and a few rolls of flab.

Jack got whacked at the optimum moment to assure his sainthood. Lies continue to swirl around his eternal flame. It's time to dislodge his urn and cast light on a few men who attended his ascent and facilitated his fall.

They were rogue cops and shakedown artists... Had one second of their lives deviated off course, American history would not exist as we know it.

It's time to demythologize an era and build a new myth from the gutter to the stars. It's time to em-brace bad men and the price they paid to secretly define our time.

Here's to them.

— JAMES ELLROY, AMERICAN TABLOID

Ellroy, best-known as the author of *L.A. Confidential* and *The Black Dahlia*, goes for the throat with *American Tabloid*[2] in a way that would make The History Channel run screaming.

This is the kind of bold confidence that captures readers. There's no fooling around. Ellroy throws his cards on the table, then kicks it over and punches you in the face while you're still trying to get up. And he does it with style, peppering in great lines like "world-class haircut" and "from the gutter to the stars."

When done right, the profound statement can be the most poetic way to open, the one that oozes atmosphere and theme, making them the star before ever showing a single character.

While the authors I've excerpted here pull off their profound statements beautifully, the longer you go with yours, the greater the odds of losing your reader. Editing the profound statement to the perfect size and focus is critical. Be ruthless!

One more thing to keep in mind is to decide whether to make your profound statement positive or negative. That gives your hero not only something to reflect on throughout your story, but something to actively fight for or against. A hero who begins believing one thing and ends up believing the opposite shows a strong character arc. They have grown from one point of view to another by taking decisive and frequently painful action.

Obviously, every hero needs an arc like this, but it becomes even more obvious (and easier to keep track of) when you begin with a profound statement. To learn more about character arcs, read my book, *The Ultimate Author's Guide to Writing Heroes & Villains.*

STORY SECRET #8

THE OTHER WAY TO BE PROFOUND

Regardless of whether you begin with a profound statement or not, see if you can work your story's theme into your opening sentence or first paragraphs. Typical themes are coming of age, conflict between individuals vs. society or technology, nostalgia (a desire to return to simpler times due to an oppressive present and likely even worse future), or the rise and fall of an individual due to personal failures—or its mirror opposite, the fall and rise, which allows for a happy ending.

While there are exceptions, it's often more effective to simply *hint* at your theme on page one and save the full-on reveal for later in your first chapter, and make sure it's a supporting or minor character who actually states the theme to your hero. The hero should either be clueless about his need for change, or else have no idea how to go about it until the other character points the way.

This mirrors how we change and grow in real life by being exposed to new people and new ideas—regardless of whether the change comes from a sudden epiphany or slow percolation, it will feel organic and honest to readers only when the inspiration comes from a source other than your hero.

CHAPTER 8 FOOTNOTES

- 1 Hagiography: a biography idealizing its subject as a saint.
- 2 From an untitled prologue to *American Tabloid.* The prior excerpt I used is from *Tabloid's* actual chapter 1.

SETTING

ONCE THE MOST COMMON WAY to open a story, setting can be tricky to make interesting. It better be a damn good (and brief) description if it's going to hook today's readers. Compare these examples with the ways I gave you before, then decide for yourself whether setting is the best way to open your story.

Darkness. Winter. A night of frost and no moon.

— BERNARD CORNWELL, SWORD SONG

You see what Cornwell is doing there in his gritty medieval adventure? No? Let's bust out another example, this time from a crime *noir* angle:

It was night. It was hot. The sea wasn't far away.

— DAY KEENE, HOME IS THE SAILOR

What do these story hooks both have in common? They both use short, choppy sentences to describe the setting. This tells the reader it is going to be a grim, nasty tale, and also an adventure—perhaps one best not taken by the hero.

You don't have to use choppy prose; you can convey the same message in one clean sentence just as easily:

> It was one of those tourist traps that have turned the coast of Florida into a glittering facade.
>
> — ROBERT EDMOND ALTER, CARNY KILL

Nice. This paints a seedy picture of a world of greed and illusion, which is exactly what the carnival in question is: a cotton candy deathtrap of sex and lies waiting for the hero to walk in...

Maybe your setting needs a slightly longer, more complex story hook. Well, we can do that too:

> The place was on the Sunset Strip, a second-floor outfit with several big-lettered banners declaring that 20 beautiful girls were on duty to massage gentlemen in private.
>
> — JIM THOMPSON, "SUNRISE AT MIDNIGHT"

Thompson serves up a sleazy location with an amusing, thinly-veiled punchline. You see why I keep coming back to him chapter after chapter? The guy's solid gold.

Like the profound statement, using setting as your story hook requires a bit more detail (and poetics) to get going, so I'll show the first two or three lines for these next examples to give you the bigger picture.

> Gold on the door, edged with black, said ALEXANDER RUSH, PRIVATE DETECTIVE. Inside, an ugly man sat tilted back in a chair, his feet on a yellow desk.
>
> — DASHIELL HAMMETT, "THE ASSISTANT MURDERER"

A classic hardboiled story hook. We can picture everything to set the stage in just two lines.

> Heidi Graham thought the woods were stupid. Stupid and boring and dumb. They surrounded her Dad's vacation cabin on all sides except for a narrow dirt road leading down the mountain. Back to civilization with its fast food and TV and boys.
>
> — JACKSON DEAN CHASE, "THE TRUTH ABOUT BIGFOOT"

Here we intro the hero by filtering the setting through her teenage angst. She wants to be back in Seattle, watching TV, fooling around with boys, not stuck in some lonely wilderness with her Dad. She hates the setting, and soon it will hate her back...

An excellent way to open with setting is to have your hero describe it in his own words. It combines monologue with setting, and allows you to get to know the hero while firmly establishing his opinions of the setting. This really puts you in there: sights, sounds, smells. Don't overlook the five senses in your descriptions! Sometimes, you may wish to emphasize only sense:

> In the period of which we speak, there reigned in the cities a stench barely conceivable to us modern men and women. The streets stank of manure, the courtyards of urine, the stairwells stank of moldering wood and rat droppings, the kitchens of spoiled cabbage and mutton fat; the unaired parlors stank of stale dust, the bedrooms of greasy sheets, damp featherbeds, and the pungently sweet aroma of chamber pots. The stench of sulfur rose from the chimneys, the stench of caustic lye from the tanneries, and from the slaughterhouses came the stench of congealed blood. People stank from sweat and unwashed clothes; from their mouths came the stench of rotting teeth, from their bellies that of onions, and from their bodies, if they were no longer young, came the stench of rancid cheese and sour milk and tumorous disease. The rivers stank, the marketplaces stank, the churches stank,

it stank beneath the bridges and in the palaces... And of course the
stench was foulest in Paris, for Paris was the largest city of France.

— PATRICK SÜSKIND, PERFUME

Get the picture? Paris stinks! We know how and we know why. It's
stated simply with a list—the details are left to the reader's imagination. By emphasizing the enormity of the problem, the author also
emphasizes the importance of perfume to mask it—which creates the
perfect segue to introduce us to the insane perfumer this novel
is about.

I lay on the lawn and watched Conrad Hickey paint a nude. She was
an Amazon with a luscious hourglass figure and skin like strawberry
juice. She looked as if she could break a man in half, and that wasn't all
she was good for.

— BRUNO FISCHER, HOUSE OF FLESH

We learn a lot in three lines. The narrator is on the lawn watching
a man paint a nude, so it must be summer. Perhaps the man is on
vacation.

Is the painter famous or merely a dabbler? We don't know, and we
get the feeling the narrator doesn't care. He only has eyes for the nude
woman, who becomes the setting, a feast for his senses that blots out
all thought of sun, grass, trees, houses. There is only this bizarre trian-
gle. Two men, each intently focused on the woman, obsessed with her
body, but for very different reasons. And like the two men, the reader
can't help but be obsessed by her.

I'm going to close out this chapter with the best description of a
setting ever written. Read it and tell me it doesn't make you desperate
to read the book!

The city could be nothing but a woman, and that's good because your
business is women.

You know her tossed head in the auburn crowns of molting autumn foliage, Riverhead, and the park. You know the ripe curve of her breast where the River Dix molds it with a flashing bolt of blue silk. Her navel winks at you from the harbor in Bethtown, and you have been intimate with the twin loins of Calm's Point and Majesta. She is a woman, and she is your woman, and in the fall she wears a perfume of mingled wood smoke and carbon dioxide, a musky, musty smell bred of her streets and of her machines and of her people.

You have known her fresh from sleep, clean and uncluttered. You have seen her naked streets, have heard the sullen murmur of the wind in the concrete canyons of Isola, have watched her come awake, alive, alive.

You have seen her dressed for work, and you have seen her dressed for play, and you have sleek and smooth as a jungle panther at night, her coat glistening with the pinpoint jewels of reflected harbor light. You have known her sultry, and petulant, and loving and hating, and defiant, and meek, and cruel and unjust, and sweet, and poignant. You know all of her moods and all of her ways.

She is big and sprawling and dirty sometimes, and sometimes she shrieks in pain, and sometimes she moans in ecstasy.

But she could be nothing but a woman, and that's good because your business is women.

You are a mugger.

— ED MCBAIN, THE MUGGER

That last line... Incredible! The whole damn thing is poetry. Beautiful. Disturbing. Seductive. This is the best use of second person point of view I've ever read. The book switches to the more accepted, respected third person point of view immediately after that. And that's fine. It's done what it needed to do: hooked the reader, landed them, and skinned them alive!

What about you? Can you write setting like this? Can you imagine it as something else? Something that ties into the theme of the story, to the hero, or as Ed McBain does, to the villain?

STORY SECRET #9

MAKE YOUR SETTING A CHARACTER

What makes a place special? Is it the sights, sounds, smells, tastes, or is it a memory, an ideal, a dream or nightmare? What strange hold does your setting have over your hero?

It's not enough to describe it, the only way to make it come alive is through the *emotional attachment* your hero has to it: Why she loves it. Why she hates it. Why she wants to never leave or can't wait to escape. Invest it with hope and heartache until your setting becomes a character and your story could happen nowhere else.

VILLAIN OR VICTIMS

NOT EVERY STORY OPENS with the hero. Some begin with the villain, just to give you a taste of how evil they are. *How insane.* How they will stop at nothing to get what they want...

Every great story needs a great villain, so it might make sense to open with one. If you do, your job is not to make him likable, but understandable, and interesting, maybe even amusing.

Assuming your villain is intelligent, there are two main types: hot and reckless or cold and logical. You need to decide which type yours will be, as they create very different feelings in the reader

Hot and reckless villains will do something impulsive, such as a crime of passion, and are unpredictable. They can be charming, to a point, but are rarely deep thinkers. It is difficult for them to change tactics, adapt to new situations, or apply pressure except through brute force.

Cold and logical villains rarely act on impulse and are deep thinkers, forever plotting their next master plan. These villains can also be charming and are quite intelligent, but their dealings with others are often undercut by arrogance, elitism, paranoia, and the like. They can apply pressure in a variety of ways limited only by circumstance and imagination.

A third type of villain would be a combination of cold and hot, perhaps switching from one to the other depending on some internal or external factor. This could be as simple as not taking their medication or being pushed too far.

You will need to give your villain some victims, but these need to be *characters readers care about*, not disposable cannon fodder. Therefore, there are three ways to open with villains:

1. You begin with the villain;
2. you begin with the victims; or
3. you begin with the hero recounting his ordeal.

When opening with the villain, it is advisable to *open with them exactly as if they were the hero*. Feel free to use any of the other successful ways to open, or you can attempt to pull off this way: a psychological study of the inner workings of the villain's mind, what drives him, what his goals and passions are. In short, telling us what kind of villain he is. In this manner, the reader comes to know not only the villain, but the type of danger he represents.

The threat posed by a maniac trucker is very different from that posed by a freewheeling con-man or rogue cop, as is the threat from an imperious alien war-princess... or a wizard, or a vampire, or a horde of mutant rats or a lone rabid dog. Well, you get the picture.

Ready? Let's delve into the minds of some villains!

A great white Kenworth[1] was gliding through the desert night. Easing the Roadranger transmission into high thirteen, the man inside lit up a cigarillo, settled in for the long haul.

He seemed sane enough, to himself—a good old boy, a trucker. They don't make 'em like that anymore. But something was wrong, terribly wrong. His eyes took on a kind of blankness, cold as the white Bonneville salt flats.

Cold as moonlight.

He reached down beside him, fondled it again. It made him feel warm. A sawed off shotgun wrapped in an old cowboy shirt.

The man loved the world of the trucker. He wanted deeply to be part of it. To that end, he had invested in his own rig. It wasn't easy to come by, but that was okay. For the trucker, just like the cowboy, nothing came easy. It was a hard life, the long haul, lonely, and the man loved it.

He had plans, many plans.

— RONALD WILCOX, THE RIG

Notice how *The Rig* begins, investing the psycho's truck with a shark-like quality by calling it a "great white." Subtle touches like this ease the reader into a disturbed state.

Our next clue something is wrong is when the villain claims, "He seemed sane enough, to himself," and then we discover he fancies himself a "good old boy, a trucker" and is a "cowboy" at heart. And "he had plans, many plans," but what do you want to bet they're all crazy or evil?

This villain is a pretender, as so many villains are, and it is his childlike desire to live out his fantasy that will cost the hero's loved ones their lives, and set the hero on a revenge-fueled collision course to destroy him.

In our next psychological profile, we have a more amusing criminal, but one who is also a pretender. He simply wants to be rich and enjoy himself, but has no compunctions about what he has to do (or who he has to kill) to get there.

Frederick J. Frenger, Jr., a blithe psychopath from California, asked the flight attendant in first class for another glass of champagne and some writing materials. She brought him a cold half-bottle, uncorked it and left it with him, and returned a few moments later with some Pan Am writing paper and a white ball point pen. For the next hour, as he sipped champagne, Freddy practiced writing the signatures of Claude L. Bytell, Ramon Mendez, and Herman T. Gotlieb.

The signatures on his collection of credit cards, driver's licenses, and other ID cards were difficult to imitate, but by the end of the hour and the champagne, when it was time for lunch—martini, small steak, baked potato, salad, chocolate cake, and two glasses of red wine— Freddy decided that he was close enough to the originals to get by.

The best way to forge a signature, he knew, was to turn it upside down and draw it instead of trying to imitate the handwriting. That was the foolproof way, if a man had the time and the privacy and was forging a document or a check. But to use stolen credit cards, he knew he had to sign charge slips casually, in front of clerks and store managers who might be alert for irregularities.

Still, close enough was usually good enough for Freddy. He was not a careful person, and a full hour was a long time for him to engage in any activity without his mind turning to something else.

— CHARLES WILLEFORD, MIAMI BLUES

What do you want to bet Freddy's going to get sloppy and end up getting himself caught or killed? Just like the maniac trucker in *The Rig*, the seeds of Freddy Frenger's destruction are planted in who he is. But that's not the only place they're planted, oh no! The seeds of destruction, the villain's Achilles' heel, if you will, are also planted in the first chapter, preferably within the first page or two as seen in *The Rig* and *Miami Blues*. It doesn't have to be obvious, but it needs to be there.

We'll mix up the psych profile approach now with monologue. That's right, we're going to hear the villain speak directly in first person to see how that changes the feel and style of the intro:

Moon. Glorious Moon. Full, fat, reddish moon, the night as light as day, the moonlight flooding down across the land and bringing joy, joy, joy. Bringing too the full-throated call of the tropical night, the soft and wild voice of the wind roaring through the hairs on your arm, the hollow wail of starlight, the teeth-grinding bellow of the moonlight off the water.

All calling to the Need. Oh, the symphonic shriek of the thousand hiding voices, the cry of the Need inside, *the entity*, the silent watcher, the cold quiet thing, the one that laughs, the Moondancer. The me that was not-me, the thing that mocked and laughed and came calling with its hunger. With the Need. And the Need was very strong now, very careful cold coiled creeping crackly cocked and ready, very strong, very much ready now—and it still waited and watched, and it made me wait and watch.

I had been watching the priest for five weeks now. The Need had been prickling and teasing and prodding me to find one, find the next, find this priest. For three weeks I had known he was it, he was next, we belonged to the Dark Passenger, he and I together. And that three weeks I had spent fighting the pressure, the growing *Need*, rising in me like a great wave that roars up on the beach and does not recede, only swells more with every tick of the bright night's clock.

But it was careful time too, time spent making sure. Not making sure of the priest, no, I was long sure of him. Time spent to be certain that it could be done right, made neat, all the corners folded, all squared away. I could not be caught, not now. I had worked too hard, too long, to make this work for me, to protect my happy little life.

And I was having too much fun to stop now.

— JEFF LINDSAY, DARKLY DREAMING DEXTER

Although Dexter Morgan is technically an anti-hero—a serial killer who only kills other killers—he still acts very much as a villain would, hiding behind a facade of normalcy and cloaking himself in a perverse sense of righteousness that what he is doing is, if not exactly good, is not exactly evil either.

Dexter has found a way to feed his beast in a way he can live with, and in a way society can live with... at least until he gets caught, which is what he lives in mortal fear of. Fortunately for him, he's as careful and meticulous as he is ruthless. And he can be quite funny at times as he tries to fit in around the office, pretending to be "human."

Dexter is cold, logical, but can get caught up in the high of the hunt, the thrill of the kill... it's the only time he ever feels truly alive, truly at peace with himself.

I've included him here because the opening is so beautifully written, so grandly poetic and pure in its evil. It could be adapted to fit any kind of cunning monster or maniac.

Let's switch genres and genders now to take a look as a female villain is introduced:

> The Tahn battle cruiser[2] arced past the dying sun. The final course was set, and in a few hours the ship would settle on the gray-white surface of Fundy—the major planetary body in the Erebus System.
>
> Erebus would seem to be the last place that any living being would want to go. Its sun was so near extinction that it cast only a feeble pale yellow light to its few heavily cratered satellites. The minerals left on those barren bodies would barely have supported a single miner. Erebus was a place to give one dreams of death.
>
> Lady Atiago listened impatiently to the radio chatter between her crew and the main port com center on Fundy. The voices on the other end seemed lazy, uncaring, without discipline—a marked contrast to the crisp string of words coming from her own crew. It grated on her Tahn sensibilities.
>
> The situation on Fundy had been neglected too long.
>
> Lady Atiago was a tall woman, towering over many of her officers. At casual glance some might think that she was exotically beautiful— long, flowing dark hair, wide black eyes, and sensuous lips. Her body was slender, but there was a hint of lushness to it. At the moment it was particularly well set off in her dress uniform: a dark green cloak, red tunic, and green form-fitting trousers.
>
> At second glance all thoughts of beauty would vanish as the chill crept up the spine. This was Tahn royalty. A nod of her head could determine any one of many fates—all of them unpleasant.
>
> — ALLAN COLE AND CHRIS BUNCH, FLEET OF THE
> DAMNED

Lady Atiago represents the cold, logical villain: haughty, entitled, arrogant. A villain smart enough, rich enough, and politically well-connected enough to remove almost anyone in her path. And she has an army willing to carry out her every command. This is the type of galaxy-spanning villain who enslaves planets—or destroys them.

Notice how the authors weave in phrases like the "dying sun," "the final course," "the gray-white surface," "feeble yellow light," "barren bodies," culminating in "a place to give one dreams of death." And of course "Erebus" is the Greek god of Darkness, the son of Chaos. Clearly, these represent death, the coldness of space, the coldness of the Tahn, their race's desire for conquest, for rigid control.

By contrast, the Fundians are described as "lazy, uncaring, without discipline" while the Tahn crew are "crisp," efficient, and presumably deadly, with imperious "sensibilities."

The authors move on to describe Lady Atiago, and at first, they go to her obvious her beauty, then her noble status, her ruthless cruelty. We know the Tahn are bad news and despite her beauty, Lady Atiago represents the worst of them.

NON-HUMAN VILLAINS

If your villain is not human or human-like, congratulations: you have your work cut out for you. But all is not lost! Many successful books open with non-human villains, such as the haunted house in *The Haunting of Hill House* by Shirley Jackson, the mutant, man-eating rats in James Herbert's *Domain*, or the rabid dog in *Cujo* by Stephen King.

> No live organism can continue for long to exist sanely under conditions of absolute reality; even larks and katydids are supposed, by some, to dream. Hill House, not sane, stood by itself against its hills, holding darkness within; it had stood for eighty years and might stand for eighty more. Within, walls continued upright, bricks met neatly, floors were firm, and doors sensibly shut; silence lay steadily against the wood and stone of Hill House, and whatever walked there, walked alone.
>
> — SHIRLEY JACKSON, THE HAUNTING OF HILL HOUSE

That's a clever way, a powerful way, to set up an inanimate object as a villain. Just one paragraph is all you need—if it's the right one. Let's take a look now at how animals might be introduced as villains:

> *They scurried through the darkness, shadowy creatures living in permanent night.*
>
> *They had learned to become still, to be the darkness, when the huge monsters roared above and filled the tunnels with thunder, assaulting the black refuge—their cold, damp sanctuary—with rushing lights and deadly crushing weight. They would cower as the ground beneath them shook, the walls around them trembled; and they would wait until the rushing thing had passed, not afraid but necessarily wary, for it was an inveterate invader but one which killed the careless.*
>
> *They had learned to keep within the confines of their underworld, to venture out only when their own comforting darkness was sistered with the darkness above. For they had a distant race-memory of an enemy, a being whose purpose was to destroy them.*
>
> — JAMES HERBERT, DOMAIN

There's more, of course. This is the third book in Herbert's immensely popular *Rats Trilogy*, and the author has to finish setting up that these are mutant rats, that the bombs have dropped, and the world is now a very different place. A place where the tables have turned, and man, the rats' most hated enemy, is now easy prey in the ruins of post-apocalyptic London.

VICTIMS

When you introduce your villain through his victims, you begin with any of the other ways to hook readers. The most critical part is that you must convince your reader that the victims matter, and are actually the heroes. Otherwise, it's just some lame *Friday the 13th* body count that does precisely zero to scare anyone.

For example, you could begin with a squabbling brother and sister:

At dusk, they finally spotted the tiny church. It was way back off the road, nearly hidden in a clump of maple trees, and if they had not found it before dark, they probably would not have found it at all.

It was the cemetery behind the church that was the objective of their journey. And they had hunted for it for nearly two hours, down one long, winding rural back road after another with ruts so deep that the bottom of the car scraped and they had to crawl along at less than fifteen miles per hour, listening to a nerve-wracking staccato spray of gravel against the fenders and sweltering the a swirl of hot, yellow dust.

They had come to lay a wreath on their father's grave. Johnny parked the car just off the road at the foot of a grassy terrace while his sister, Barbara, looked over at him and breathed a sigh intended to convey a mixture of happiness and relief.

Johnny said nothing. He merely tugged angrily at the knot of his already loosened tie and stared straight ahead at the windshield, which was nearly opaque with dust.

— JOHN RUSSO, NIGHT OF THE LIVING DEAD

After some sibling drama, they lay the wreath, then the villain appears... the first of many, only Johnny and Barbara don't recognize the danger they are in.

In the distance, a strange moving shadow appeared, almost as a huddled figure moving among the graves.

Johnny and Barbara dismiss the "strange moving shadow" as the caretaker, and go on arguing. About the past. About the present. And soon, none of it matters, because the man is there, and he's not the caretaker at all. He's a walking corpse!

And suddenly, the man grabbed Barbara around the throat and was choking her and ripping at her clothes.

Johnny comes to his sister's defense, but only succeeds in getting himself killed. Barbara runs off in a panic, pursued by the shambling zombie. She locks herself in an isolated farmhouse that becomes surrounded by the living dead!

Although Barbara doesn't die, she does descend into a near useless, semi-catatonic state. The real hero, Ben, shows up and sets about trying to save them both. It's up to him to explain what's going on and the nature of the enemy—as well as how to destroy them. That's important.

The victims don't understand what's going on at first, and that's as it should be. This sets the stage for the hero to come in and look like he knows what's going on and what to do.

When you lead with victims, you want readers wondering about things that don't matter, like who will the fight between Johnny and Barbara? Which one is right?

Night of the Living Dead is a famous example, but an even more famous one is *Psycho*. I'm specifically talking about the 1960 Alfred Hitchcock film, rather than the Robert Bloch novel it was based on.

The novel opens with Norman Bates; the movie opens with Marian Crane as the greatest throwaway victim of all time. We spend a good twenty minutes getting to know Marian as she plots to steal the company payroll and run off to Mexico. And she might have gotten away with it too, if she hadn't stopped for the night at the Bates Motel. There, she's promptly stabbed to death in the shower by Norman's "mother."

If you'd like to study more on the subject of throwaway victims, I recommend you read the *Novelist's Essential Guide to Crafting Scenes* by Raymond Obstfeld (chapter 10).

RECOUNTING THE ORDEAL

The third way to introduce the villain is where the hero takes on the role of victim to recount his ordeal, desperately trying to work it all out in his mind. This segues into the point it all began, creating a frame device[3] where we start in the present, then return to the past to experience the villain in action. Once the villain is defeated, we may or may not return to the hero in the present. If the last image is powerful enough, there is no reason to.

Gil Brewer used this technique in his novel, *A Killer Is Loose*, in which hotheaded psycho Ralph Angers decides to "befriend" the hero and drag him along on his one-man killing spree.

Looking back, the hero has this to say:

> If I can get all of this straight and true, and get Ralph Angers down here the way he really was, then I'll be happy. It's not going to be easy. There was nothing simple about Angers, except maybe the Godlike way he had of doing things. He was some guy, all right. In the news lately, you've read of men doing some of these things, like Angers. They were all red-hot under the same cold star when the wires snapped and Death became a pygmy. So I figure I better get this told. There are plenty of Ralph Angers now on the streets, on the trains, in the bars, in the hotels, in the houses, at the ball game, and there's no way to tell who, until it happens. Hell, no. So this is my story and how it happened with me, and how it ended. It ended simply, come to think of it. I guess it had to.
>
> — GIL BREWER, A KILLER IS LOOSE

We then launch into the hero's day, that first day, the day he met Ralph Angers. The day his life changed forever. But we don't meet Ralph right away, not until twenty pages in, and even then, we don't get his name until after he blows a bartender's head off. That's when he introduces himself and asks the hero his name. As if everything's normal. As if there isn't a dead man on the floor. *As if the hero is his new best friend.* I'd hate to see what happened to his old ones!

Here's another example of the hero recounting his ordeal, this time from one of my favorite horror stories:

> Fate plays strange tricks on one, doesn't it? Six months ago I was a well-known and modestly successful practicing psychiatrist; today I

am an inmate of a sanatorium for mental cases. In my capacity of of alienist and physician I have often committed patients to the selfsame institution in which I myself am now confined, and today—irony of ironies!—I find myself their brother in misfortune.

And yet I am not really mad. They sent me here because I chose to tell the truth, and it was not the kind of truth men dare reveal or recognize.I acknowledge that my part in the matter led me to suffer a severe nervous breakdown, but it did not derange me. My story is true; I swear it—but they will not believe. Of course I really have no substantial proof to offer; I have never seenProfessor Chapin since that eventful night last August, and my subsequent investigations failed to substantiate his claim to a post at Newberry College. This, however, only testifies to the validity of my statement; a statement which sent me to shameful confinement, to a living death I abhor.

There is one other concrete proof which I could give if I dared, but that would be too terrible. I must not lead them to the exact spot in that nameless cemetery and point out the passage that yawns beneath that tomb. It is better that I should suffer alone, that the world at large be spared the knowledge that destroys sanity. Yet it is hard for me to live like this, and to the drabness of my days my nighted dreams add endless torment. That is why I choose to set down this account— perhaps the unfolding of my own story will serve somehow to ease the painful burden of my memory.

— ROBERT BLOCH, "THE GRINNING GHOUL"

The villain, Professor Chaupin, is introduced in the very next paragraph, but he comes as a patient, complaining of bad dreams that have their origin in a certain cemetery... Eventually, Chaupin convinces the hero to accompany him there, if only to disprove that his nightmares are real. And, this being a horror story, not only are his dreams real, but there is a shocking twist to them I dare not reveal here.

STORY SECRET #10

NOBODY THINKS THEY'RE EVIL

Every villain is the hero of his own story. He will rationalize all the horrible things he does in order to justify to himself and anyone who will listen that "there was no other choice." Sure, he may acknowledge some choices were difficult, and might even express regret, but will still insist what he did was for "the greater good" and that "the ends justifies the means." To do otherwise would mean confronting who he is as a person, what he has become, and that's painful.

EVIL COMES FROM PAIN

Keep in mind evil comes from damage, from deep pain and unresolved trauma. After all, if the villain wasn't suffering, he wouldn't feel the need to lash out and bring pain to others.

That pain, that inner torment, is not easily addressed. Any attempt to do so will be met with suspicion, paranoia, anger. The villain's brain has created defenses against pain, and unfortunately, those defenses are expressed in "evil" ways.

REDEEMING THE VILLAIN

Some villains can be redeemed. Some of the most powerful storytelling involves a hero redeeming his nemesis, such as Luke Skywalker redeeming Darth Vader in *Return of the Jedi*. Depending on how far the villain has fallen, he may need to sacrifice himself against some greater evil, as Vader does by attacking the Emperor.

Note that Vader does this for selfish reasons—to save his son's life—not because he cares for the Rebel Alliance. He still believes in the Empire, but *his version of it...* a version with himself as Emperor and Luke as his prince and heir, his second-in-command.

Consider how the end of *Return of the Jedi* would play out if Vader did not die after killing the Emperor. He would take command of the Death Star and either continue the Emperor's plan to destroy the

Rebel fleet, or offer some sort of truce or compromise in order to secure Luke's loyalty and buy himself time to complete the Death Star's construction. He would no doubt try to get Luke to act as an intermediary between him and the Rebels.

How would Luke react? How would the Rebels respond?

Another option exists, and that is for the redeemed villain not to die (though he will still need to make some form of sacrifice or atonement) to achieve redemption. Consider the storytelling possibilities: the hero and villain can team up, perhaps permanently, perhaps temporarily. They might even become lovers—which could be the cause for them staying together, or the cause for them breaking apart. Batman and Catwoman come to mind as an example of this.

Instead of becoming friends (or at least *friendly*), they might become rivals rather than remain enemies. There are fun options to consider there as well. Think about it...

The former villain could reject some (not all) of the hero's morality, and become an anti-hero, which might feel more comfortable after having lived inside a villain's skin for so long. Perhaps the hero has to work hard to keep his overenthusiastic new "friend and ally" on the right path.

For more about how to write villains, read my companion book, *The Ultimate Author's Guide to Writing Heroes & Villains*.

∿

CHAPTER 10 FOOTNOTES

- 1 Opening with vehicles can be problematic—people identify with people over objects. In this case, the truck is an extension of the villain, so this is an exception.
- 2 The starship is an extension of the villain. It is also used to set up everything else leading to the villain walking onstage. I prefer the Admiral Lar Ventesh example in Chapter 11.
- 3 Frame devices are discussed in Chapter 16.

II

THE TEN WAYS NO STORY SHOULD BEGIN

(AND HOW TO FIX THEM)

Learn how to "break the rules"
with examples from bestselling authors

WARNING!

THE NEXT TEN WAYS are the *wrong ways* to open your story. They are so bad, lazy, or outdated that you will have agents, editors, and readers cursing your name before they finish the first sentence. And they're even worse when you combine them in the same opening.

LEARN THE RULES BEFORE YOU BREAK THEM

"But Jackson," I'm sure some of you are saying, "it's really important that my story opens with a dream, or a phone call, or the weather." Maybe it is. Probably it isn't. But hey, I get it. You want to be creative, and you're itching to prove me wrong.

But just hang on a moment. First, let me show you *why* each of these ten ways are terrible, then I'll show you how to "fix" them. And not just fix them so they're "all right," but so they're super-awesome and you look like a genius.

That doesn't necessarily mean I recommend you use these next ten ways—especially if you're just starting out—but I want to provide you with as many options as possible.

—JDC

ANTIQUATED WRITING STYLE, TECHNOBABBLE, ETC.

The first act of hostility of old Duke Balthasar towards the Snake Lady, in whose existence he did not, of course, believe, was connected with the arrival at Luna of certain tapestries after the designs of the famous Monsieur Le Brun, a present from his Most Christian Majesty King Lewis the XIV.

— VERNON LEE, "PRINCE ALBERIC AND THE SNAKE LADY"

DID YOU ENJOY READING THAT? I sure didn't. And the story goes on in that same antiquated style for thirty-eight pages! Sadly, it doesn't matter how good the underlying story might be if no one will sit still long enough to read it. Today's readers want historical fiction to be told in a lively, modern manner that's easily understood.

HOW TO FIX IT

If you insist on using this kind of opening, a reasonable compromise would be to use a *slightly* antiquated style in your first paragraph (but keep it brief), then ease into modern structure in your second. For example:

In the year of Grace 1150, when the ungodly Saracens, the scum of the earth and the vanguard of the Antichrist, inflicted many defeats on our forces in the Holy Land, the Holy Spirit descended upon Frau Sigrid and gave her a vision which changed her life.

Perhaps it could also be said that this vision had the effect of shortening her life. What is certain is that she was never the same again.

—Jan Guillou, *The Road to Jerusalem*

Do you see how that gets the *flavor* of ancient times across but reads so much easier than "Prince Alberic" did? Get in and get out. I can't stress that enough. But the simplest solution is to avoid an antiquated style altogether. Instead, *talk* about antiquated or archaic things, like reading omens:

The gods talk by signs. It may be a leaf falling in summer, the cry of a dying beast or the ripple of wind on calm water. It might be smoke lying close to the ground, a rift in the clouds or the flight of a bird.

But on that day, the gods sent a storm. It was a great storm, a storm that would be remembered, though folk did not name the year by that storm. Instead they called it the Year the Stranger Came.

For a stranger came to Ratharryn on that day of the storm. It was a summer's day, the same day Saban was almost murdered by his half-brother.

The gods were not talking that day. They were screaming.

— BERNARD CORNWELL, STONEHENGE

This does what we want in a clean, modern voice. There's no risk of alienating readers by dipping into an antiquated style, and it immediately grips you: *Gods. Omens. Storms. Murder.* Bernard Cornwell is considered the greatest living writer of historical fiction for a reason, and it's not just because he's a prolific bestseller. It's because he knows how to tell an exciting story from start to finish!

Regarding antiquated words, names, or phrases: You can slip them into your story every now and again if you must, but they should be easy to pronounce and understand. And no, including a glossary, pronunciation guide, or historical notes won't let you off the hook.

FOREIGN, ALIEN, OR FANTASY LANGUAGES

Foreign languages present a similar problem, regardless of whether they are antiquated or modern. Again, use them sparingly and go for short words, curses, or phrases most people have heard of that are easy to translate into English: *Madre de Dios!*, *Nyet*, *Was ist das?*, etc.

Alien or fantasy languages adhere to this same rule. Use them sparingly, and make it obvious what they mean, either through implication or direct translation.

For example:

Gravka, Red Olath thought, glaring at the outlanders. *Fools.*

In this case, it is obvious "fools" is the direct translation of "gravka" from his native tongue. See how closely that translation follows the first appearance of the fantasy word? That's to make sure it's clear to readers. It also implies the character is fluent in both tongues, but English (or your world's equivalent) is not the language of his people.

<<*Mystel don'du,*>> the alien said, and a moment later, my voice-com translated the words as, "We come in peace."

Alien, fantasy, or foreign languages which are spoken aloud may be stylized as such by wrapping them with << >> instead of the customary double quotation marks. This is purely an aesthetic style option, and by no means a requirement.

CURSES

Starting with a curse can be a colorful way to begin. To be effective, curses should be repeated often throughout the story. For example,

Battlestar Galactica uses "frak" instead of the "F" word, and *Farscape* uses "frell." Harry Dresden, star of urban fantasy author Jim Butcher's *Dresden Files* series, often mutters, "Stars and stones!"

Conan the Barbarian frequently mutters, "Crom!" (the name of his god), but it seems to be a universal word (not always a curse) that could imply awe, contempt, disgust, resignation, surprise, triumph, and just about any other emotion the author wants. It's meaning at the time is in the context of the scene.

Other times in Conan's life call for more colorful curses, usually invoking animals or gods:

- "By the black beard of Set!"
- "Hanuman's stones!"
- "Spawn of a jackal!"

Similarly, not an episode of TV's *Thundarr the Barbarian* went by without that post-apocalyptic hero exclaiming, "Demon dogs!" or "Lords of Light!" What kind of colorful curses can you come up with to bring your world to life?

TECHNOBABBLE

This is when instead of opening with antiquated language, you open with its opposite: specialized technical jargon (such as in a police procedural) or futuristic jargon.

A good example of technobabble can be found in *Star Trek* and other science fiction. Here's an example of how NOT to open your sci-fi novel:

The Makari battle cruiser *Logadon* warped into the Hox'li Geminar System at precisely 89:15 IGT (Intergalactic Time). She was a big ship, sleek and deadly, sporting a full array of Ardon phase cannons in the recently approved Sekk-4 configuration.

Um, what the what now? This is what you get when you try to cram too much information into one paragraph, then further cripple reader comprehension by sprinkling in made-up alien language along with a new method for measuring time. No thanks.

This type of opening can quickly overwhelm readers, particularly casual ones. It is not reasonable for you to expect them to learn more than a few abbreviations, technical terms, or anything else in the course of a single story, much less in a single paragraph!

Let's rewrite this, simplifying the language and technobabble, breaking it up over multiple paragraphs to ease readers in:

> Admiral Lar Ventesh paced the bridge of the *Logadon*. The battle cruiser was a big ship, sleek and deadly, bristling with weapons. Weapons waiting to be used, as the admiral waited to be used, called into action by the Makari High Command.
>
> Should war come, the Hox'li Geminar System was the target. An outback system, unimportant but for the fact it lay on the border of the Makari empire.

Better, right? We now lead with the hero (or possibly the villain), because readers identify with people before objects. We cut out the IGT, the Ardon phase cannons, and the Sekk-4 configuration. We were forced to add an alien name for the admiral, but that's OK. We still improved reader comprehension, especially by moving the Hox'li Geminar System to the second paragraph.

Could we make it better still? Absolutely.

> *War is coming. War and death, blood and conquest.*
>
> Admiral Lar Ventesh paced the bridge of the *Logadon*. The battle cruiser was a big ship, sleek and deadly, bristling with weapons. Weapons waiting to be used, as the admiral waited to be used, called into action by the Makari High Command.
>
> Should war come, the Hox'li Geminar System was the target. An outback system, unimportant but for the fact it lay on the border of the Makari empire.
>
> *The empire needs expanding.* Everyone on the home world said so, as

did the High Command. Admiral Ventesh, however, was not so sure. It was not that he was afraid to die, or to cause others to die—he was responsible for the deaths of thousands, including his own son—but the reason mattered. It had to be for the greater good, not the greater greed.

Admit it, Lar, he thought. *You're getting old.* Only an old man wonders about his legacy, about the kind of universe he leaves behind...

"Sir!" the com-officer shouted. "Incoming message from High Command: Priority One!"

Ventesh gave the officer a curt nod. "Patch it through to my quarters." He turned and stalked away, knowing war had come.

Now instead of opening with action (pacing the bridge), we open with monologue, the admiral's private thoughts. This tells us war is coming. But what kind of war, and who will wage it? Admiral Lar Ventesh of the Makari Empire, that's who!

Lar is an older man concerned about his legacy, concerned about the heart and soul of his empire. A conflicted man, yet we have no doubt he is competent, that he cares deeply, and that he bears the responsibility for the death of his son. We can guess he is going to come into conflict not just with the Hox'li Geminar, but with his own High Command, and that this will have a huge impact on the course of the story. All this from one page—the first page.

Notice I did not add any more made-up words or technobabble to the extra paragraphs. *It's critical to space that stuff out.* Introduce the bare minimum, then save the rest for later. There is no hard limit per chapter, but I would be cautious going over five or six new words or terms, and even that might be pushing it.

12

CORRESPONDENCE OR DIARY

Jonathan Harker's Journal

3 May. Bistritz. Left Munich at 8:35 P.M., on 1st May, arriving at Vienna early next morning; should have arrived at 6:46, but train was an hour late. Budapest seems a wonderful place, from the glimpse which I got of it from the train and the little I could walk through the streets. I feared to go very far from the station, as we had arrived late and would start as near the correct time as possible.

The impression I had was that we were leaving the West and entering the East; the most western of splendid bridges over the Danube, which is here of noble width and depth, took us among the traditions of Turkish rule.

We left in pretty good time, and came after nightfall to Klausenburgh. Here I stopped for the night at the Hotel Royale. I had for dinner, or rather supper, a chicken done up some way with red pepper, which was very good but thirsty. (Mem. get recipe for Mina.) I asked the waiter, and he said it was called "paprika hendl," and that, as it was a national dish, I should be able to get it anywhere along the Carpathians.

— BRAM STOKER, DRACULA

IT'S GENERALLY A BAD IDEA to open with correspondence of any kind. Even a diary or journal can be tricky. Especially if you're trying to replicate the antiquated speech of the past or including technical jargon, colloquialisms, or anything else that may confuse or annoy readers.

This doesn't mean you can never include them in the your story. A few bits of brief *and* story-driven correspondence can be a welcome break from the rest of the text—and even expected, such as texting in a Young Adult novel. But only in moderation, as a necessary part of the story, and *as far from the opening as possible*. That's because correspondence creates barriers:

1. The first barrier is the format itself. Reading anything that it is not in the expected fiction format looks like work. Like most people, I read fiction to escape. To put it another way, I work all day. I don't want to have to work for my entertainment as well.

2. The second barrier is the impression of emotional distance formal correspondence or dry journals can give. We don't know the characters yet, haven't seen into their hearts and souls (let alone actions), so we can't possibly care what they have to say. After all, if I was interested in reading random communications from strangers, I'd be a secretary or computer hacker.

Maybe you think because several famous novels either began with or consisted solely of correspondence[1], you can get away with it too. Maybe you can, but I wouldn't count on it.

Let's take a closer look at the example from *Dracula*: it's boring. Nothing happens![2] The most exciting event is the discovery of paprika. If this novel were about a Victorian spice hunter instead of vampires, then *maybe* it would have some value.

As written, there's nothing there. No hook, no suspense, no insight into who Jonathan Harker is, not even what he's doing in Transylvania. It's a terrible way to open![3]

HOW TO FIX IT

Do you only need a little correspondence to start your story? That's easily solved when you make it the hook:

> The postcard came in Friday's mail. Squires read it while he was waiting for dinner:
>
> *Hiya Partner!*
>
> *I'm back in the old home town for a few days, revisiting old haunts. Am staying at the Maplecrest. Hope you can find time to drop in and see me.*
>
> *Yours,*
>
> *—Guy*
>
> Squires read the words again. He couldn't remember ever having known anyone named Guy.
>
> The card was the pictureless kind carried by the post office. It bore a local postmark and had been mailed the day before. Both the address and the message had been printed in uneven block letters with a soft-lead pencil. The name "Guy" was similarly printed.
>
> Some crank, probably.
>
> He consigned the card to the part of Friday's mail that was destined for the wastebasket. At once it vanished from his mind and did not return 'til early Monday morning when the phone rang. His wife, Adeline, answered it; he was in the upstairs bathroom, shaving. "It's for you, Nick," she called from the downstairs hall. "Someone named Guy."
>
> — ROBERT F. YOUNG, "YOURS,—GUY"

See how nice this is? The postcard is the mystery that creates the hint of danger. It's short, and set off the rest of the text in italics. You could do the same thing with an email, text, or instant message.

In his bestselling YA novel, *Thirteen Reasons Why*, Jay Asher does this with audio tapes. His hero, Clay Jensen, receives a package from a girl at his school who committed suicide. The tapes inside were recorded by her before she killed herself and promise to reveal the "thirteen reasons why[4]" she did it. Naturally, she sends Clay running all over town to track down clues and solve the mystery.

As you can see, a little correspondence goes a long way. But do you need any at all? Rather than include it in the text, could you paraphrase it instead? Let's see how to handle that in the following example from the amusingly titled memoir, *Flat Broke with Two Goats*:

> I was upstairs folding laundry when I hear the horn. From the wide porch window, I watched a blue car with a flashing yellow light on top ease around the bend—the mailman. Our mailbox stood next to the main road, almost a mile away from the house, and because our driveway was full of holes and bumps and sagging telephone wires, most delivery people left our packages there, wedged against the mailbox flag. In fact, since out move here to the woods, we had only had one other group of unexpected visitors, Jehovah's Witnesses who sprang from their car, stuck a leaflet on a window ledge, and were gone before I could get to the door.
>
> So I knew the mailman's presence meant only one thing: certified mail. And I knew that certified mail meant only one thing: bad news.
>
> — JENNIFER MCGAHA, FLAT BROKE WITH TWO GOATS

I'm going to skip ahead a few paragraphs here, past the initial setup, to when the author opens her certified letter:

> Inside the cabin, I opened the envelope from the attorney. The papers outlined everything I already knew, skipping a few of the more salient points, such as how irresponsible and short-sighted we were for entering into a contract where our friends, Jeff and Denise, had owner-financed our home.

That's all we get of the correspondence. The author launches into detail about *her* reasons for why the situation didn't work out (debt problems), which is a convenient way to fill in the backstory without it feeling like an info-dump.

DIARIES

For me, an all-correspondence ("epistolary") novel is a cheap gimmick and creative dead-end. I won't write 'em, won't read 'em. But when done right (not like *Dracula*), diaries are an exception. They are the opposite of correspondence because they are *meant* to be intimate and revealing. Here's an example from the author of *Psycho*:

> First off, I want to write that I never did anything wrong. Not to nobody. They got no call to shut me up here, whoever they are. They got no reason to do what I'm afraid they're going to do, either.
>
> I think they're coming pretty soon, because they've been gone outside a long time. Digging, I guess, in that old well. Looking for a gate, I heard. Not a regular gate, of course, but something else.
>
> Got a notion what they mean and I'm scared.
>
> I'd look out the windows but of course they are boarded up so I can't see.
>
> But I turned on the lamp, and found this here notebook so I want to put it all down. Then if I get a chance maybe I can send it to somebody who can help me. Or maybe somebody will find it. Anyway, it's better to write it out as best I can instead of just sitting here and waiting. Waiting for *them* to come and get me.
>
> — ROBERT BLOCH, "NOTEBOOK FOUND IN A
> DESERTED HOUSE"

Unlike Bram Stoker, Robert Bloch doesn't waste time. We know his hero is in danger from the first paragraph[5].

No discussion of diaries would be complete without reviewing two of the most famous (and infamous): *The Basketball Diaries* by Jim Carroll, and *Go Ask Alice* by Anonymous. These work for the same reason "Notebook Found in a Deserted House" does—they let you into the heart and head of the hero so quickly you don't have a choice but to like them. And once you like them, you're hooked!

Fall '63

Today was my first Biddy League game and my first day in any organized league. I'm enthused about life due to this exciting event. The Biddy League is a league for anyone 12 yrs. or under. I'm actually 13 but my coach Lefty gave me a fake birth certificate. Lefty is a great guy; he picks us up for games in his station wagon and always buys us tons of food. I'm too young to understand about homosexuals but I think Lefty is one. Although he's a great ballplayer and a strong guy, he likes to do funny things to you like put his hand between your legs and pick you up. When he did this I got keenly suspicious. I guess I better not tell my mother about it.

— JIM CARROLL, THE BASKETBALL DIARIES

Notice the hint of danger present, and how easily the hero accepts lying and breaking the rules. This is the beginning of his descent into darkness, drugs, and crime.

September 16

Yesterday I remember thinking I was the happiest person in the whole earth, in all of God's creation. Could that only have been yesterday or was it endless light-years ago? I was thinking that the grass had never smelled grassier, the sky had never seemed so high. Now it's all smashed down upon my head and I wish I could just melt into the blaaaa-ness of the universe and cease to exist. Oh, why, why, why can't I? How can I face Sharon and Debbie and the rest of the kids? How can I? By now the word has gotten around the whole school, I know it has! Yesterday I bought this diary because I thought at last I'd have something wonderful and great and worthwhile to say, something so personal that I wouldn't be able to share it with another living person, only myself. Now like everything else in my life, it has become so much nothing.

— ANONYMOUS, GO ASK ALICE

Again, we have the hint of danger—word about what has gotten around school? How much pain and humiliation will be heaped upon this hero's head beyond what she's already tortured herself with, and what happens when she reaches the breaking point?

So to recap, if you're going to open with correspondence, make sure it's the best way to begin (even better if it's the only way), and don't waste time. Dig right into the hero's heart and head, make us know and love them, make us fear for them, and give us a sense of time and place either through the text itself or via headers like "Fall '63" or "September 16."

~

CHAPTER 2 FOOTNOTES

- 1 When an entire book is constructed of correspondence, it is called the "epistolary format," an eighteenth-century literary device that unfortunately keeps being resurrected just like Dracula.
- 2 Read more about why this is one of the wrong ways to open in Chapter 14: Nothing Happens.
- 3 That does not mean *Dracula* isn't a great *concept*. Clearly, the ideas in Stoker's novel hooked generations of fans and were a major influence on the horror genre.
- 4 There's that title synergy I keep talking about. See how much fun it is?
- 5 The diary gimmick is right there in the title and adds a strong sense of mystery. What happened to the guy who wrote the notebook? Why did he leave it in the house? You'll have to read the rest of the story to find out...

13

DREAM OR FLASHBACK

It's hard being the princess of a small country. And a beauty queen. And a movie star. Just the other day, Fabio was over and I told him to put my star on the Hollywood Walk of Fame because I just can't be bothered. Fabio said he would, then turned into a unicorn with glittery wings and flew away. It was then that my alarm went off and I was nobody again.

— ANONYMOUS TERRIBLE AUTHOR

OPENING WITH A DREAM OR FLASHBACK makes the reader feel cheated. Still feel the need? Well, there's always an exception.

HOW TO FIX IT

The only acceptable way to open with a dream or flashback is not to hide it, and never to extend it past the first sentence. What's more, it must have some profound impact on your story as it unfolds, whether literally or as a metaphor.

Here's an example:

I was dreaming of sea monsters when the phone rang.

— LAURELL K. HAMILTON, "A SCARCITY OF LAKE
MONSTERS"

Of course, this is opening with two no-no's, combining waking up *and* a phone call, but because the author ties it to such a weird, intriguing dream, it becomes a successful exception.

How did Hamilton do it? First, she let us know it was a dream, so there's no way the reader can feel deceived. Then she said the dream was about sea monsters, which intrigued us, then she had the phone ring to explain why the dream ended.

This transition makes us annoyed the phone rang because we want to find out more about the dream. Which is the point. Hamilton hooks us with visions of Loch Ness, then delays telling us more about the dream so we can find out about the main character instead.

If she had gone into more detail about the dream first, she would have lost us. You keep readers hooked by delaying gratification til the last possible second. This builds suspense, the most crucial of story ingredients.

Let's look at another example:

It began with a shattered dream.

— DAVID GOODIS, OF TENDER SIN

A *noir* master, Goodis gets right to the point. The dream is a poetic metaphor for the soon to be shattered life of the main character through drug addiction and a tragic affair. His full opening reads:

It began with a shattered dream. The winter night was suddenly real and Alvin Darby was wide awake, seeing the darkness of the bedroom, the January whiteness beyond the window, then the wispy whiteness of the blanket that covered his wife in the adjoining twin bed. He took all that in to assure himself he was truly awake. He lifted his fingers and applied pressure to his cheekbones, wanting to be doubly sure. But the contents of his mind did not seem to be wakeful thoughts. He had a feeling that someone uninvited had entered the house.

This is a complicated opening paragraph that combines three no-no's (dream, waking up, and weather), but adds setting and premonition. It works for the same reason that the previous example did. Instead of sea monsters and phone calls, Goodis distracts us with weather, with setting, with a man unsure of his own reality, then hits us with a psychic warning of danger.

The weather in particular ("whiteness") serves as a metaphor for how empty Alvin finds his marriage and his life. He is restless, wanting more, and soon he will find it—with terrible consequences. The uninvited visitor is another metaphor for his dissatisfaction and urge to do something about it.

Here's "Big" Jim Thompson again with his version of how to open with a dream:

> He had dreamed about her. Now waking to the sweaty southern night, he found both arms clasped around his pillow, the cloth wet with saliva where his mouth had pressed against it, and he flung it away from him with a mixture of disgust and amusement. Some babe, he thought drowsily, his hand moving from the bed lamp to alarm clock to cigarettes. A dream boat—and that's the way he'd better leave her. Right in the land of dreams. He had to keep the money coming in. He had to keep out of trouble. And he had been sternly advised, at the time of his employment by the Hotel Manton, that bellboys who attempted intimacies with lady guests invariably landed in serious trouble.
>
> — JIM THOMPSON, A SWELL-LOOKING BABE

This dream defines the hero's goal, all his arguments against pursuing it, and leaves us with the certain knowledge that even if he wanted to, the hero could not stop himself from getting tangled up with his "dream girl."

The entire plot (minus all the fun twists and surprises) has just been handed to us and we're grateful, knowing the author is going to deliver the thrills we expect.

But what if you want to spend more time in the dream? Well, there are ways to do that:

> In the dream, I find myself alone in a room. I hear musical chimes—a sort of music box tune—and I look around to see where the sound is coming from.
>
> "I'm in a bedroom. Heavy curtains close off the windows, and it's quite dark, but I can sense that the furnishings are entirely antique— late Victorian, I think. There's a large four-poster bed, with its curtains drawn. Beside the bed is a small night table upon which a candle is burning. It is from here that the music seems to be coming.
>
> "I walk across the room toward the bed, and as I stand beside it I see a gold watch resting on the night table next to the candlestick. The music-box tune is coming from the watch, I realize. It's one of those old pocket-watch affairs with a case that opens. The case is open now, and I see that the watch's hands are almost at midnight. I sense that on the inside of the watchcase there will be a picture, and I pick up the watch to see whose picture it is.
>
> "The picture is obscured with a red smear. It's blood.
>
> "I look up in sudden fear. From the bed, a hand is pulling aside the curtain.
>
> "That's when I wake up."
>
> — KARL EDWARD WAGNER, "BEYOND ANY MEASURE"

Rather than being an actual dream, Wagner wisely has his hero recall his dream's contents to a psychiatrist. You could do the same thing with your hero via hypnosis, a support group meeting, even over drinks with a friend.

FLASHBACKS

Let's move on to flashbacks to see how blockbuster author John Grisham handles them in the opening to one of his legal thrillers:

> My decision to become a lawyer was irrevocably sealed when I realized my father hated the legal profession. I was a young teenager, clumsy, embarrassed by my awkwardness, frustrated with life, horrified of puberty, about to be shipped off to a military school by my father for insubordination. He was an ex-Marine who believed boys should live by the crack of the whip. I'd developed a quick tongue and an aversion to discipline, and his solution was simply to send me away. It was years before I forgave him.
>
> He was also an industrial engineer who worked seventy hours a week for a company that made, among many other items, ladders. Because he handled design, my father was the favorite choice to speak for the company in depositions and trials. I can't say I blame him for hating lawyers, but I grew to admire them because they made his life so miserable. He'd spend eight hours haggling with them, then hit the martinis as soon as he walked in the door. No hellos. No hugs. No dinner. Just an hour or so of continuous bitching while he slugged down four martinis then passed out in his battered recliner. One trial lasted three weeks, and when it ended with a large verdict against the company my mother called a doctor and they hid him in a hospital for a month.
>
> — JOHN GRISHAM, THE RAINMAKER

This flashback paints a vivid portrait of the hero's complicated relationship with his father. You come away with a perfect understanding of the forces that shaped the hero both as a man and a lawyer. You like him because he's a clever underdog who rose up and got the better of his cruel father, and you expect he'll find a way to do the same to the villains he's about to fight in the courtroom.

Before we end this chapter, I want to share my quick and dirty technique for how to make dreams and flashbacks work using the "Get In and Get Out" story secret from the Premonition chapter.

Here's a couple first lines I wrote as examples:

In my dream, I'm falling into a deep, dark hole. The worst part is, I wake up in one.

Or what about this?

I remember the day the meteor hit. Life's been hard ever since.

The first sentence sets up the past, the second brings us into the present. Both must be exciting. There's no lingering, or need to.

Whatever the most important dream or flashback detail is goes in the first sentence. If there are other details, slot them in later, as far away from the opening as possible. Make it about the present, but in the context of the dream or flashback's effect on the hero's life.

NOTHING HAPPENS

Joe Drummond did his job. Just like every day. He drank coffee and smoked cigarettes and typed reports at Conglom Industries. If he kept at it, he might get promoted in a few years. That was something Joe thought about as he ate his hamburger lunch and spaghetti dinner.

Joe was the best report writer in the whole company. Everyone knew it. He'd even won the report writing contest last month. Boy, that had been a swell moment. He had the plaque on his wall where it held the place of honor next to his diploma from Franklin University where Joe had been the star quarterback.

Ah, good old F.U.! Those were great times, glory days, but they belonged to the past. As the days went by, Joe wrote more reports and won more contests...

— ANONYMOUS TERRIBLE AUTHOR

SERIOUSLY? Nobody cares! Fiction is not real life—don't try to write it that way. Everything has to happen for a reason, and that reason is either to deepen our understanding of the characters and their situation, or to drive the plot forward. In fiction, things never happen "just because," or "that's the way it happens in real life."

HOW TO FIX IT

Poor Anonymous Terrible Author[1]! There's no way to fix this except to *make something happen*. Isn't that why you decided to write fiction in the first place? To tell exciting stories? Well, you can't do that if nobody gets past your first chapter, let alone your first paragraph. If that's you, go back to the beginning of this book, pick one of the right ways and start over.

I feel like I'm writing the end to one of those old Choose Your Own Adventure™ stories—the kind where you screwed up and died. Fortunately, there's still hope!

CHAPTER 4 FOOTNOTES

- 1 *Surprise!* I'm the "Anonymous Terrible Author" throughout this book, writing fake excerpts to illustrate my point. And also so as not to offend any living authors by calling them out...

PHONE CALL

Ring! Ring! I put down my mop and hurried to answer the phone. "Hello? Janitor Jim speaking. Have mop, will travel!"

— ANONYMOUS TERRIBLE AUTHOR

PHONE CALLS ARE GREAT WAYS to deliver news, but not when they're used to open your story. Too many authors have tried and it's beyond stale. It's even worse combined with the hero waking up.

HOW TO FIX IT

My basic advice is never open with an actual phone conversation, and avoid the stupid *"Ring! Ring!"* sound effect—that's a rookie move.

Can a phone call successfully start a novel? Possibly, *if* you combine it with action or mystery in an unusual way.[1]

Mark sat on the edge of his bed and stared at the telephone.

— RICHARD LAYMON, FRIDAY NIGHT IN BEAST HOUSE

Wait! That's not a very interesting opening line, you say. Well, that's true, but it's setting up something that is. Did you notice Mark is not answering or making a phone call in this sentence?

That's because the opening is about Mark psyching himself up to call Alison, the girl of his dreams, and ask her on a date. But instead of jumping right to that, the author delays reader gratification by making Mark suffer, going over all the reasons why he thinks Alison will (or won't) say yes. Which means we get to go deep into Mark's thoughts and find out a lot about him before he ever makes the call—which happens on page four of Laymon's novel, by the way.

What does Mark's suffering look like? Well, about like you'd expect it would, but the thing Laymon does is alternate between the positive and negative to create tension. It's all about yes/no, yes/no:

Do it! Don't be such a wuss! Just pick up the phone and dial.

He'd been telling himself that very thing for more than half an hour. Still, there he sat, sweating and gazing at the phone.

Come on, man! The worst that can happen is she says no.

No, he thought. That's isn't the worst. The worst is if she laughs and says, "You must be out of your mind. What on earth would ever possess you to think I might consider going out with a complete loser like you?"

She won't say that, he told himself. Why would she? Only a real bitch would say a thing like that, and she's…

…wonderful…

To Mark, everything about Alison was wonderful. Her hair smelled like an autumn wind. Her face, so fresh and sweet and cute that the very thought of it made Mark ache. The mischief and fire in her eyes. Her wide and friendly smile. The crooked upper tooth in front. Her rich voice and laugh. Her slender body. The jaunty bounce in her step.

He sighed.

She'll never go out with me.

The phone is a symbol for Mark's fear and desire, a dangerous door into the unknown. Picking it up and dialing Alison's number will change Mark's life, for better or worse. The phone almost becomes another character, as the postcard does in the excerpt from "Yours,— Guy" in the Correspondence chapter.

The trick to a successful phone opening is to use it an unexpected way. Here are some quick examples I made up to illustrate my point:

Lisa Miller picked up the phone in one hand and the gun in the other.

Not bad. Here the phone implies the threat of calling in the cavalry: police, an angry boyfriend, or maybe her lover's wife! The fact she's got a gun too tells us she means business.

But what if the hero doesn't have a gun? Who says they need one when they can just the phone *as* a weapon? Or maybe just have it active in the scene...

The phone was still ringing as Bill Johnson beat the man to death.

OK, maybe you don't want to open with *that kind* of phone action. Why not use the phone as a mundane action to segue to drama?

I was programming my new cell phone when Dad told me about the divorce.

The action could take on significance later if programming the phone turns out to be important to the story—maybe the hero finds a mysterious app preinstalled that promises to help her parents get back together...

There's another fun way to open with a phone, and that's as the delivery vehicle for mystery, horror, or adventure:

When I answered the phone, my dead mother was on the line.[2]

This last example breaks the rules by having the hero answer her phone, but it's all right, because you know it's not going to be a normal conversation. How can it be? There's a ghost on the other end!

You could have it be an alien, a monster, a wizard, a secret agent, a cop, a celebrity, or anyone, as long they are instantly identifiable as unusual.

All these phone hooks feature unexpected twists, and that's what you should be aiming for in yours.

~

CHAPTER 5 FOOTNOTES

- 1 Also refer to how Laurell K. Hamilton does it in "A Scarcity of Lake Monsters" in Chapter 13: Dream or Flashback.
- 2 Ghostly or threatening phone calls have served as the basis for a number of excellent thrillers over the years, including *Sorry, Wrong Number, When Michael Calls, When a Stranger Calls,* and *Phone Booth.*

PROLOGUE OR FRAME

Lest anyone think my claim to the throne of Merlinia illegitimate, let it be known that I was born Princess Rayzine of House Kordell. I was stolen by gypsies from the royal crib and spirited away to Goblin Town.

— ANONYMOUS TERRIBLE AUTHOR

PROLOGUES ARE DANGEROUS. Bad writers have abused them as a way to info-dump backstory and series recaps, or to front-load action to cover a boring first chapter.[1]

HOW TO FIX IT

Opening with a prologue may make the reader skip it because they think it's pointless or contains spoilers. The most obvious way around the problem is to change the name from "Prologue" to "Chapter One," "Before," "Winter 1970," "Planet Septor Prime," "Spain, 1492," etc. This could be a one-off trick just to disguise the prologue, or you can repeat it as a device to allow cutaways to the villain or other characters operating away from the hero.

Does changing a prologue's name solve the problem? With most readers, sure. But the truth is, no matter what you do, some people will always skip anything that isn't labeled "chapter one" (unless none of your chapters are numbered, then they don't have a choice).

So if prologues are such a problem, why should you write one? Because sometimes the story demands it. In the right hands, a good prologue can be an incredibly useful tool to quickly establish all kinds of things in your novel: the hero's past, defining what the current (or most recent) state of "normal" is for the hero's world. It's also a way to show the villain without having to put the hero in danger—yet.[2]

But what exactly is a prologue? Why all the reader hate, and why do so many authors get it wrong? One of my favorite writing gurus, Jeff Gerke, said it best in his classic book, *The First 50 Pages*[3]:

> Think of a prologue as a short story. Make it a standalone narrative that would work as a complete little story unto itself. The opening sequence in *Indiana Jones and the Last Crusade* is a great example… It takes place independently of the main story but has bearing on it.
>
> — JEFF GERKE, THE FIRST 50 PAGES

There! That was easy. A prologue is a short story that adds value and meaning to the main story, but also works without it. The best example I can think of is the beginning of the James Bond films, where we join our hero at the climax of his most recent mission. *Bang! Bang!* Bad guys die. The main titles roll, then we see Bond back at head-quarters getting his next assignment. Which means talking, and talking is boring to action fans. That's why Bond films always start with action.

Taking it a step further, in the Bond film, *Goldeneye*, the prologue *is* related to the main plot. We see Bond teamed up with another secret agent. Something bad happens to the second agent, Bond completes the mission, and then we cut to the usual mission briefing. Only it turns out Bond's former teammate, feeling betrayed at how the last mission went down, is now the villain and Bond's next assignment!

THE UNLABELED PROLOGUE

There's another trick clever authors use to get around prologue hate, but it requires your prologue to fit on one page (and preferably about half that). Because it's unlabeled, prologue haters don't have any preconceived notions about it, though they might still skip it.

This type of prologue works best as a mystery, premonition, or profound statement, but I'm sure you can get creative and make anything work if you try hard enough.

Here's how it works:

> People disappear all the time. Ask any policeman. Better yet, ask any journalist. Disappearances are bread-and-butter to journalists.
>
> Young girls run away from home. Young children stray from their parents and are never seen again. Housewives reach the end of their tether and take the grocery money and a taxi to the station. International financiers change their names and vanish into the smoke of imported cigars.
>
> Many of the lost will be found, eventually, dead or alive. Disappearances, after all, have explanations.
>
> Usually.
>
> — DIANA GABALDON, OUTLANDER

This sets up the runaway theme as well as the expectation the hero will either disappear or be a journalist investigating a mysterious disappearance (and maybe disappear herself). The fact it's a time travel romance adds that extra twist.

Carrying on with the theme of the unlabeled prologue, Gabaldon begins her first chapter like this:

> It wasn't a very likely place for disappearances, at least at first glance.

You see how chapter one's hook complements the unlabeled prologue? *One builds on the other.* That's important. That's why it works. If the author had switched to an unrelated subject in her first line, it would have negated the beauty of her prologue.

FRAMES

A frame is a specific form of prologue that includes a matched set of prologue and epilogue[4] that must mirror each other. This is almost always a flash forward where the novel begins long after the main story has been resolved. The main story is introduced by a narrator who may or may not be an older version of the hero or someone from the hero's past—perhaps a best friend, lover, or even the villain himself! The hero may or may not be dead at this point (see the 1949 film noir, *D.O.A.*, for an example of a dead hero telling his story). If the hero is the one presenting the story, he may choose to hide this fact from the reader until the end.

Two great examples of the frame device can be found in the films *Amadeus*, narrated by the villain, and *Titanic*, narrated by the hero.

Take a look at *Conan the Barbarian* (1982) and *Mad Max 2: The Road Warrior* (1981), which both have an unnamed, offscreen narrator set up the world and the hero. When the narrators return for the epilogue (again offscreen), we learn who they are in relation to the hero, and what happens after the main story is resolved.

After the main story ends, the epilogue returns us to the narrator in the future. He wraps up his tale and reveals what effect it had on his life... and perhaps yours.

Sometimes the narrator interrupts the main story with cutaways back to him telling the story throughout the book, but other times, there is no more mention of the narrator again until the end. Both of these present problems.

Like prologues, readers may resent (and skip) cutaways that take them out of the main story's timeline. The problem with not having cutaways is that by the time readers get to the epilogue, they may have forgotten about the prologue and be confused or angry at having to go back and re-read it to gain a full understanding of the epilogue.

A frame doesn't have to be a standard full chapter, and sometimes, it's better if it isn't because readers will be less likely to skip it. Here's one of the most famous examples of a short frame:

> Know, O prince, that between the years when the oceans drank Atlantis and the gleaming cities, and the years of the rise of the Sons of Aryas, there was an Age undreamed of, when shining kingdoms lay spread across the world like blue mantles beneath the stars—Nemedia, Ophir, Brythunia, Hyperborea, Zamora with its dark-haired women and towers of spider-haunted mystery, Zingara with its chivalry, Koth that bordered on the pastoral lands of Shem, Stygia with its shadow-guarded tombs, Hyrkania, whose riders wore steel and silk and gold. But the proudest kingdom of the world was Aquilonia, reigning supreme in the dreaming west.
>
> Hither came Conan the Cimmerian, black-haired, sullen-eyed, sword in hand, a thief, a reaver, a slayer, with gigantic melancholies and gigantic mirth, to tread the jeweled thrones of the Earth under his sandaled feet.
>
> — ROBERT E. HOWARD, "THE PHOENIX ON THE SWORD"

The formula is simple: the first paragraph establishes your world, the second introduces your hero. You're in and out in half-a-page. Even prologue haters may be inclined to read something this short!

Still think that's too long? The 1982 Conan film abbreviates Howard's opening still further:

> Between the time when the oceans drank Atlantis, and the rise of the Sons of Aryas, there was an age undreamed of. And unto this, Conan —destined to bear the jeweled crown of Aquilonia upon a troubled brow.
>
> It is I, his chronicler, who alone can tell thee of his saga. Let me tell you of the days of high adventure!
>
> — CONAN THE BARBARIAN (1982)

When you come back at the end, as the Conan film does, you simply give a quick wrap-up while teasing adventures to come:

> So did Conan return the wayward daughter of King Osric to her home, and having no further concern, he and his companions sought adventure in the West. Many wars and feuds did Conan fight; honor and fear were heaped upon his name.
>
> In time, he became a king by his own hand... This story shall also be told!

Here's another example of a short frame; this one is labeled as "Before" instead of "Prologue."

> Hallowell High:
>
> You're either someone or you're not.
>
> I was someone. I was Regina Afton. I was Anna Morrison's best friend. These weren't small things, and despite what you may think, at the time they were worth keeping my mouth shut for.
>
> — COURTNEY SUMMERS, SOME GIRLS ARE

The rest of the novel functions as one long flashback, beginning at a wild high school party the night everything spins out of control.

Like *Conan the Barbarian*, the purpose of this frame is to let readers know who the hero is, her primary location (Hallowell High), and that she is the spoiled, stuck-up sidekick to the school's queen bee. It's also clear the hero is about to undertake a painful transformation. What's unclear is whether she ends up alive or dead. This creates a nice, disturbing tone—a tone that says, "Look out! This story is dark."

Using the frame as a short summary technique serves as a useful shorthand that cuts out the need for complicated backstory later. In a few paragraphs, you instantly familiarize readers with your hero and her world as well as your story's theme, tone, and genre.

Keep your prologues and frames short and you can't go wrong.

~

CHAPTER 6 FOOTNOTES

- 1 See Chapter 17: Telling or Info-Dumping.
- 2 In his must-read book, *The Novelist's Essential Guide to Crafting Scenes*, writing guru Raymond Obstfeld shows you how to create sympathetic and engaging "victims" for your prologues. Remember, the reader still has to *care* for the victim if what the villain does to them is to have any meaning. Think of poor Marian Crane getting stabbed to death in *Psycho,* or Conan's brave, loving parents cruelly murdered before his eyes in *Conan the Barbarian* (1982).
- 3 *The First 50 Pages* by Jeff Gerke is a fantastic resource that features an excellent chapter on composing first lines, as well as first pages and beyond (up to the first fifty, as the title implies). I highly recommend it!
- 4 Unlike prologues, epilogues are read by most readers and don't provoke the same blind hatred.

TELLING OR INFO-DUMPING

Peggy Malloy felt rotten.

— ANONYMOUS TERRIBLE AUTHOR

OH, REALLY? I feel rotten too after reading that line. *Telling* is summary, a shortcut to speed your story along past the boring parts to get to the exciting stuff. *Showing* is making scenes stand out by putting extra attention on them—in enough detail so the reader can infer what's happening without the author having to summarize it for them. There's no good way to open with telling. Don't do it!

HOW TO FIX IT

Here's how I turn the above example into showing:

Peggy Malloy cursed the rain. She cursed her drunken husband, Tom, fired today from his third job this year. She cursed the ache in her gut and the hole in her roof. If one more thing went wrong, she didn't know what she was going to do. Scream, probably, but that wasn't

Peggy's biggest fear. Her biggest fear was once she began, she might never stop.

This *shows* Peggy feeling rotten. It's obvious and helps us get to know the hero through her thoughts and feelings, so it feels organic and honest.

INFO-DUMPS

An info-dump, on the other hand, is telling on steroids. It's where the author dumps a bunch of boring information he *thinks* is important on the reader. Unfortunately, the reader doesn't care and skips over the information or throws the book away in frustration. Even brilliant books by bestselling authors are sometimes guilty of this.

For example, I love the *The Pillars of the Earth* by Ken Follett. It's a medieval epic about the hard lives of people building a cathedral. Note that I said it's about the *people*. Unfortunately, at one point in an otherwise perfect novel, Follett devotes merciless pages to describing the intricacies of building techniques. And I skip it, because I signed up to read about horrible, gritty lives, not get a Ph.D in medieval architecture.

Yet there are many other instances throughout *The Pillars of the Earth* where medieval building techniques are discussed, and I didn't skip those. In fact, I read them with interest. What's the difference? Three things:

1. the details were kept brief;
2. they were carefully sprinkled over multiple chapters via multiple conversations; and
3. they were all presented as *problems* involving plot points.

For example, the heroes need stone to build a bridge (one of several massive construction projects undertaken throughout the course of the novel). The closest place to get it is from a quarry owned by friendly monks, but the monks require convincing. Talking about the stone and why it's important, how to cut and transport it, and why it must be done soon takes up several conversations, and not just from the heroes' side, but the villains' as well.

Read how Ken Follett handles it as his villains decide how to stop the heroes:

> "My brother feels he must accept the authority of the prior of Kingsbridge," Ralph said to Earl Roland on his return. Before the earl had time to get angry, he added: "But there may be a better way to delay the building of the bridge. The priory's quarry is in the heart of your earldom, between Shiring and Earlscastle."
>
> "But it belongs to the monks," Roland growled. "The king gave it to them centuries ago. We can't stop them taking stone."
>
> "You could tax them, though," Ralph said. ..."They will be transporting their stone through your earldom. Their heavy carts will wear away your roads and churn up your river fords. They ought to pay."
>
> "They'll squeal like pigs. They'll go the king."
>
> "Let them," Ralph said, sounding more confident than he felt. "It will take time. There are only two months left of this year's building season—they have to stop work before the first frost. With luck, you could delay the start of the bridge until next year."
>
> Roland gave Ralph a hard look. "I may have underestimated you," he said. ..."But how shall we enforce this tax? Usually there's a crossroads, a ford in a river, some place every cart has to pass through."
>
> "Since we're only interested in blocks of stone, we could simply camp a troop of men outside the quarry."
>
> "Excellent," said the earl. "And you can lead them."

— KEN FOLLETT, THE PILLARS OF THE EARTH

The information is never forced on readers all at once, and we only learn enough to move the story forward, always with the promise of either diplomatic or physical action to pay off the new knowledge. It also raises new questions while answering old ones.

Suppose you can't make the "conversation sprinkling" method work, and you have a lot of information you need to get across fast. There is a way, but it's tricky. This technique is called, "The Pope in the Pool," and it was first coined by screenwriter Blake Snyder in his influential screenplay writing guide, *Save the Cat!*:

> "...the Pope in the Pool gives us something to look at that takes the sting out of telling us what we need to know. And does so in a lively and entertaining way."
>
> — BLAKE SNYDER, SAVE THE CAT!

What this means is you must *distract* the reader from what you're really doing. You do this by presenting the info in an unusual setting or under conditions so unexpected or compelling that the reader never recognizes the scene for the info-dump it is.

In Snyder's example, the Pope is swimming laps in the Vatican pool when he is delivered information from one of his underlings. Because we've never seen the Pope in his bathing suit, let alone knew the Vatican had a swimming pool, we're immediately distracted by what's going on. It's not a static scene with two men sitting around talking.

The Pope continues to swim as the guy tells him what's going on, and we can break up his dialogue with the Pope's actions, thoughts, feelings, and replies, the sound of the water, the room's acoustics, etc. The setting becomes a third character, and the way the information is delivered is altered to accommodate this unusual setting.

It doesn't have to be the Pope in a pool. It could be the villain torturing a victim in his dungeon while his trusty henchman reports on the hero's progress. It could be a wizard in the middle of a dangerous experiment being interrupted by his apprentice while all kinds of strange spirits and glowing symbols float around him.

Other ideas: crack houses, opium dens, racetracks, sewers, a massage parlor, a space cantina full of aliens, etc. See what I mean? The only limits are your imagination.

LISTS

Lists are a specific form of info-dump rarely seen anymore, but still worth mentioning. They are a cheap and lazy way to shortcut your setup:

> Manfred, Prince of Otranto, had one son and one daughter: the latter, a most beautiful virgin, aged eighteen, was called Matilda. Conrad, the son, was three years younger, a homely youth, sickly, and of no promising disposition; yet he was the darling of his father, who never showed any symptoms of affection to Matilda. Manfred had contracted a marriage for his son with the Marquis of Vicenza's daughter, Isabella; and she had already been delivered by her guardians into the hands of Manfred, that he might celebrate the wedding as soon as Conrad's infirm state of health would permit.
>
> — HORACE WALPOLE, THE CASTLE OF OTRANTO

Granted, you could rewrite this to make it more modern, but it would still be a poor way to open. There's no hook. Though convenient, lists don't work because the reader does not yet care about anything or anyone presented in the list. The extensive nature of lists prevent the reader from focusing on any one person or detail. Rather than clarify, they overwhelm the reader with information they don't need to know (at least, not yet) and are quickly forgotten.

The only way to fix lists is not to include them. Instead, find organic ways to weave the info in. This may take several pages or several chapters, but regardless, your reader will thank you for it.

18

UNLIKABLE OR FLAT HERO

Lester Lossen was in a hurry to get to his psychiatrist's office. He'd had a bad morning and, just as he was about to leave the house, an attack of nervous diarrhea had set him back twenty minutes. Now, the traffic was murdering him. He weaved in and out the lanes, farting so bad he had to roll down the windows to get some relief.

A Dodge Neon got in his way and he cut it off, flashing the startled driver the finger when she hit her horn.

"Screw you!" Lester screamed. "Burn in hell!"

All these stupid people, Lester thought. God ought to give 'em the plague. Just wipe 'em out. He hoped the doctor would renew his prescriptions. Not that he'd been taking them. Lester sold his psych meds to high school kids. He needed the money to fund his next "get rich quick" scheme, the one that would swindle the crippled old ladies at the nursing home where he worked out of their life savings.

Lester made a left-hand turn into the psychiatrist's lot and parked in the handicapped space. He reached into the glove box and hung the disabled placard he'd stolen from one of his patients from the rearview mirror. He watched it dangle with a satisfied grin.

— ANONYMOUS TERRIBLE AUTHOR

As AMUSING as this may be, can you imagine anyone wanting to spend hours, perhaps days or weeks of their lives reading about Lester? He doesn't have a single redeeming quality, not even the *hint* of one buried deep down. He's hateful and greedy, and only out for himself. There's no way he can carry a novel.

Don't let this happen to you! Flat heroes from Caspar Milquetoast to Superman are also a problem because they put readers to sleep. They're either not good at anything or *too good* at everything. Your hero must be flawed to be interesting and his flaws must help create or at least influence a whole story's worth of interesting problems. And don't forget to give your hero quirks! Real people are walking contradictions.

HOW TO FIX IT

One easy fix for an unlikable or flat hero is to assign three things he's good at, and three things he's not. Have him screw up and be embarrassed. Make him an underdog.

You may not be able to show all his positive and negative qualities in chapter one, nor do you necessarily want to. What you do want to do is *humanize* your hero as much as possible. Sure, he's going to be clueless about needing to change, or else have no idea how to do it, but whatever event is going to initiate that change must happen to him by the end of chapter one.

Let's get back to Lester and see how giving him some redeeming qualities changes how readers respond:

> Lester Lossen was in a hurry to get to his psychiatrist's office. He'd had a bad morning and, just as he was about to leave the house, an attack of nervous diarrhea had set him back twenty minutes. Now, the traffic was murdering him. He weaved in and out the lanes, farting so bad he had to roll down the windows to get some relief.
>
> He was so busy with the window he accidentally cut a lady in a Dodge Neon off. The startled driver leaned on her horn.

"Sorry!" Lester shouted. The driver flashed him the finger and Lester sped off, changing lanes to get away from her.

All these angry people, Lester thought. *Road rage. Riots.* What was the world coming to when no one could be civilized, let alone accept an apology?

He hoped the doctor would renew his prescriptions. Not that he'd been taking them. Lester gave them to his sick mother, told her they were for her heart condition. She had a lot of problems (Lester didn't like to use the term, "crazy," though that's what everyone else in the family called her, and why he was the only one who would take her in). As for Mother, she didn't believe she had any problems—except Lester—and refused to see a psychiatrist.

The pills he'd been giving her were helping, but not enough. She still managed to throw a fit at least once a week, and always over some little thing he could never predict. After her last tantrum had sent Lester to the emergency room with a black eye, he'd begun to regret opening his home to her. That regret had turned into something else last month when the letter from the insurance company came. It said that Mother was worth a hundred thousand dollars to him dead. Now, Lester wasn't sure what she was worth to him alive, and that bothered him. It kept gnawing at him every time Mother pissed herself or babbled about the "shadow people" living in the walls.

Lester sighed as he made a left-hand turn into the psychiatrist's parking lot. All the spaces were full except the handicapped one. He took it, pulling Mother's disabled placard out of the glove compartment and hanging it from the rearview mirror. He watched it dangle, almost took it down, then said, "Screw it. Just this once won't hurt."

See how much better this reads? Unlike the first example, Lester is not presented as a two-dimensional cartoon character, but a real, hurting human being. Sure, he's flawed and does some bad things, but he isn't malevolent, and hasn't done anything unforgivable yet. The difference in this version is we see him starting to go down a dark path, but not so evil yet he's beyond redemption.

19

WAKING UP

It was six o'clock when the alarm clock woke Sally Jones from a sound sleep. She yawned, stretched, and got out of bed. Bacon and eggs were cooking downstairs. Sally slipped into her homespun robe and comfy slippers then went to go eat.

"Oh goody," Sally said. "Breakfast is my favorite!"

Her husband, Jim, smiled. "Especially when you don't have to cook it."

She stuck out her tongue, then looked out the window. The sun was up, the birds were singing. It was a perfect day. Nothing could spoil it.

— ANONYMOUS TERRIBLE AUTHOR

Boring! It doesn't matter how a character wakes up (from a dream, nightmare, loud noise, etc.). It's rarely if ever a good way to open a story, and it's at its worst when you combine it with "nothing happens," as in the example above. A surprising number of first-time authors try to open with their main character waking up to a normal, boring day, and then take *forever* for anything exciting to happen. Don't be one of them!

HOW TO FIX IT

Like any rule, there are exceptions, such as when the main character has amnesia and starts as a blank slate, or when something exciting is taking place, combining waking up with action or mystery to hook the reader.

Here are two quick ideas to see what I'm talking about:

I woke to the screams of my wife dying.

Janet woke beside a stranger.

In her blockbuster dystopian novel, *The Hunger Games*, Suzanne Collins merges waking with references to dreams:

> When I wake up, the other side of the bed is cold. My fingers stretch out, seeking Prim's warmth but finding only the rough canvas cover of the mattress. She must have had bad dreams and climbed in with our mother. Of course she did. This is the day of the reaping.

— SUZANNE COLLINS, THE HUNGER GAMES

Similarly, the sequel to *Divergent* begins with Veronica Roth's hero waking up:

> I wake with his name in my mouth.
> *Will.*
> Before I open my eyes, I watch him crumple to the pavement again. Dead.
> My doing.

— VERONICA ROTH, INSURGENT

Not to be outdone, YA author James Dashner gets in on the act in his *Maze Runner* sequel:

She spoke to him before the world fell apart.

Hey, are you still asleep?

Thomas shifted in his bed, felt a darkness around him like air turned solid, pressing in. At first he panicked; his eyes snapped open as he imagined himself back in the Box–that horrible cube of cold metal that had delivered him to the Glade and the Maze. But there was a faint light, and lumps of dim shadow gradually emerged throughout the huge room. Bunk beds. Dressers. The soft breaths and gurgly snores of boys deep in slumber.

Relief filled him. He was safe now, rescued and delivered to this dormitory. No more worries. No more Grievers. No more death.

Tom?

A voice in his head. A girl's. Not audible, not visible. But he heard it all the same…

— JAMES DASHNER, THE SCORCH TRIALS

Telepathy is an unusual way to wake up, so that's why this works. It infuses a sense of mystery and the hint of danger that is otherwise missing from the hero's seemingly safe surroundings.

What if your hero is just a regular guy living in the real world? Can you still open with him waking up? Yes and no, but you better make it fast, and you better tie it into some kind of mystery or danger… or dangerous mystery. Yeah, that's even better!

A sudden banging on the front door sent a chill down my neck and into my chest. It was two-thirty in the morning. I was up and out of my bed immediately, though still more than half asleep.

I had to go to the bathroom but the knocking was insistent; seven quick raps, then a pause, and then seven more. It reminded me of something but I was too confused to remember what.

"All right," I called out.

I considered staying quiet until the unwanted visitor gave up and left. But what if it was a thief? Maybe he was knocking to see if there was anybody home. If I stayed quiet he might just break the two-dollar lock and come in on me. I'm a small man, so even if he was just your run-of-the-mill sneak thief he might have broken my neck before realizing that Paris Minton's Florence Avenue Book Shop didn't have any money in the cash box.

— WALTER MOSELEY, FEAR ITSELF

Here, we see a small man, a nervous man, jolted out of bed by an unknown visitor. He's confused, half asleep and afraid, unsure what to do. Mystery author Walter Moseley takes full advantage of the opportunity the knock brings to delay the hero's response long enough for us to get to know him. This backstory about the hero and his shop goes on a few more paragraphs before the hero answers the door.

I opened the door and Fearless Jones strode in, wearing a green suit with a white shirt, no tie, no hat, and dark shoes. The tip of the baby finger on his left hand was missing, shot off in a gunfight that almost got us both killed, and he had the slightest limp from a knife wound he'd received saving my life in San Francisco many years before.

Fearless was tall, dark, and handsome, but mostly he was powerful. He was stronger than any man I'd ever known, and his will was indomitable. Fearless wasn't a smart man. A twelve-year-0old might have been a better reader, but if he ever looked in your eyes he would know more about your character than any psychiatrist, detective, or priest.

"I'm in trouble, Paris," we said together.

Fearless grinned but I didn't.

The visitor turns out to be the hero's old friend, so readers can breathe a sigh of relief the danger isn't immediate. The problem (and why the hero isn't exactly happy to see him) is that when Fearless Jones knocks, trouble is never far behind. So now we know that not only is poor Paris unlikely to get back to sleep, he's also about to share in whatever misfortune Fearless has gotten into. This is mitigated slightly by the fact we immediately like Fearless; we know he's a good guy, a fair guy, and not just tough. Precisely the kind of qualities that can get a man into trouble in this crooked, messed-up world...

Remember, when you open with your hero waking up, you must find a way to make it special, exciting, dangerous.

GOING TO BED

Instead of opening with your hero waking up, try its opposite, going to bed:

I was about to hit the sheets when the volcano blew.

When Hank stumbled home drunk, he never expected to find a dead girl in his bed.

Do you see the potential of this angle? Here's how one of my favorite authors opens with his hero desperate for sleep:

Ralph stood on the corner, leaning against the brick wall of Silver's candy store, telling himself to go home and get some sleep. It was half-past two in the morning and he should have been in bed long ago. The December wind hacked at his face and seemed to slice through his flesh, like saw-toothed blades biting away at his bones. He kept telling himself to go home and slide under a warm quilt. But somehow he couldn't move away from the corner. He was staring at the blonde woman on the other side of the street.

— DAVID GOODIS, THE BLONDE ON THE STREET
CORNER

Goodis sucks you in, planting you firmly in Ralph's shoes. You know where Ralph is, what he should do, and why he can't. The blonde. That damn blonde! More important than sleep, more important than shelter. She has a hold on Ralph, and that obsession will destroy him. We get all that in one paragraph, along with some nice synergy with the title.

Because a thousand other authors haven't begun with their hero going to bed, it's still a fresh enough concept that you can get away with it. Of course, the rest of the rules for how to open your story still apply. You can't have your hero go to bed and dream, or have nothing happen. He has to be *actively prevented* from falling asleep, if he even makes it home. You then use that tension, that tired frustration, to make things worse for your hero.

For example, how much worse is it to defend against a zombie apocalypse when you haven't slept in twenty-four hours? How much harder is it to avoid snapping at your co-workers or spouse when you're tired?

Or, instead of being ready for bed, what if your hero is drunk? Or high? Or physically or mentally ill? Any altered state that encourages bad decisions can increase tension.

WEATHER

THE MOST MALIGNED and made fun of opening of all time is one reason why you should never open with weather:[1]

It was a dark and stormy night; the rain fell in torrents—except at occasional intervals, when it was checked by a violent gust of wind which swept up the streets (for it is in London that our scene lies), rattling along the housetops, and fiercely agitating the scanty flame of the lamps that struggled against the darkness.

— EDWARD BULWER-LYTTON, PAUL CLIFFORD

LIKE SETTING, weather tends to bore readers, so if you insist on using it, you better make damn sure it's unusual in some way and adds something to the story. Combining it with setting, premonition, and/or monologue tend to produce the best results, but whatever you do, make sure you're done talking about it in one sentence or one paragraph at most. At that point, if you have not introduced your main character already, it's time to do so. Fast.

Here are some successful examples of weather used to open

stories, and I've allowed them to go on for up to a paragraph to give you a better idea why they work:

> It rains a lot, up here; there are winter days when it doesn't really get light at all, only a bright, indeterminate gray. But then there are days when it's like they whip aside a curtain to flash you 3 minutes of sunlit, suspended mountain, the trademark at the start of God's own movie.
>
> — WILLIAM GIBSON, "THE WINTER MARKET"

Gibson evokes sad, bittersweet feelings of love and loss in a grand poetic style.

> They had been predicting a norther all week and along about Thursday we got it, a real screamer that piled up eight inches by four in the afternoon and showed no signs of slowing down.
>
> — STEPHEN KING, "GRAY MATTER"

This weather traps the hero in a rapidly worsening situation. As a writer, you should always be asking yourself, "How can I make things worse for my characters?" Well, a blizzard is one way to do it—and in the first sentence too!

And speaking of blizzards, here's how to really show the effect extreme weather can have on your hero:

> The winter that Zebulon set his traps along the Gila River had been colder and longer than any he had experienced, leaving him with two frost-bitten toes, an arrow wound in his shoulder from a Crow war party, and to top it all off, the unexpected arrival of two frozen figures stumbling more dead than alive into his cabin in the middle of a spring blizzard.
>
> Rather than waking him, the cold blast of wind from the open door became part of a recurrent dream: a long endless fall through an

empty sky toward a storm-tossed sea... *Come closer*, the towering waves howled...

— RUDOLPH WURLITZER, THE DROP EDGE OF YONDER

As you can see from this wild west example (loosely adapted into the 1996 Johnny Depp film, *Dead Man*), it's not the weather itself, but its effect on the hero that makes it such a surprisingly good hook.

Weather doesn't have to extreme to have an emotional impact on the hero:

Nobody ever walked across the bridge, not on a night like this. The rain was misty enough to be fog-like, a cold gray curtain that separated me from the pale ovals of white that were faces behind the steamed-up windows of the cars that hissed past. Even the brilliance that was Manhattan by night was reduced to a few sleepy, yellow lights off in the distance.

— MICKEY SPILLANE, ONE LONELY NIGHT

The hero is telling us about a specific, weather-related exception to the usual traffic at the location. If nobody ever walks across the bridge on a night like this, then what dark thoughts or need are compelling the narrator to brave the weather? Is he going to jump? Or is he meeting someone?

There were no street lamps, no lights at all. It was a narrow street in the Port Richmond section of Philadelphia. From the nearby Delaware, a cold wind came lancing in, telling all alley cats they'd better find a heated cellar. The late November gusts rattled against midnight-darkened windows, and stabbed at the eyes of the fallen man in the street.

— DAVID GOODIS, SHOOT THE PIANO PLAYER

Here we have the city as character affected by weather. It builds to the final line revealing what appears to be a dead body lying in the street. Masterful.

> There was a desert wind blowing that night. It was one of those hot dry Santa Anas that come down from through the mountain passes and curl your hair and make your nerves jump and your skin itch. On nights like that, every booze party ends in a fight.
>
> — RAYMOND CHANDLER, "RED WIND"

This opening works because:

1. the Santa Ana winds are exotic, well-known, and tied to a specific location; and
2. the weather is interpreted through the cynical mind of Philip Marlowe, private eye. It's not just describing the weather, it's describing the mood.

Here's another example of weather being used to convey the season as well as a strong sense of place:

> It was spring in Yoyogi Park, and not a rain, exactly. Cool mist floated in the air, drawn to the heat of a thousand milling bodies, clinging to all the things that lived: girl groups dressed in black lace and garters, thirty young boys dressed up as James Dean, pompadours and chains and black leather jackets.
>
> — NANCY HOLDER, "CAFE ENDLESS: SPRING RAIN"

In one superb paragraph, we go from weather to the ethereal effect it has on the characters.

You can even get all poetic and literary (even a touch folksy) if you're careful:

Midsummer: The long days begin in bright, rising mist and never end. Their hours stretch, they stretch. They stretch to hold everything you can shove into them; they'll take whatever you've got. Action, no action, good ideas, bad ideas, talk, love, trouble, every kind of lie— they'll hold them all. Work? No. Nobody works any longer. To be sure, they did. The farmers worked. The midsummer days were the best working time of the year for the farmers, but the farmers are gone. They worked, they built, but they're gone. Who's next?

— CASTLE FREEMAN, JR., GO WITH ME

This is one of the greatest openings of all time. It sets the mood, the place, the season. It lets you know you are in the hands of a master, but like the Nancy Holder "Cafe Endless" example above, where is it going? The next paragraph reveals that:

Sheriff Ripley Wingate, an early riser, turned off the road and into the lot behind the courthouse. Not yet seven. The morning fog still hung to the ground, a heavy gray curtain. It shifted, wavered, passed in woolly swags and swirls, parted. Nearly hidden in the mist, in a corner of the lot, another vehicle, a little car, empty.

Or is it? As Sheriff Wingate is about to discover, the car is not only *not* empty, but contains the hero. She's in a bad state, after having just had her cat murdered by his deranged ex-deputy, Richard Blackway. What will the sheriff do? Well, given that this is a thriller, we can start guessing.

This superb 2008 novel was made into *Blackway*, a 2015 film starring Anthony Hopkins.

Let's go now from the backwoods of modern day Vermont to the backwoods of a fantasy kingdom to see how weather (again, mist) can play a crucial role building mystery:

Damn mist. It gets in your eyes, so you can't see no more than a few strides ahead. It gets in your ears, so you can't hear nothing, and when you do you can't tell where it's coming from. It gets up your nose, so you can't smell naught but wet and damp. Damn mist. It's a curse on a scout.

— JOE ABERCROMBIE, BEFORE THEY ARE HANGED

This is a wonderful way to open that sets the mood and wilderness location through the havoc the weather is playing on the hero. Only in the final line is the narrator revealed to be a scout, so we can assume whoever (or whatever) he's scouting is about to get the jump on him.

Another successful way to open with weather in fantasy is if the hero is summoning it, or bearing witness to someone attempting the same:

It was a hot summer, dry and deadly. A summer of wilted crops and wilted hope. And so it was with great reluctance that the village elders came to me and begged for rain.[2]

We instantly get a sense of the weather's effect on the location, that this is not a modern setting, and that the hero either has (or is believed to have) the ability to change the weather. We also know magic is thought to be a last resort and thus assume the hero is an outsider, a witch or native shaman of some kind.

Here's another example, this time with a villain or anti-hero:

Lenore felt the sky split. The heavens opened, not just to her magic, but to her will. A will strengthened by hate, nurtured by malice. The clouds darkened, thunder and lightning becoming allies, rain and wind the deadliest of friends. Now, let the fools suffer! Now, let them burn and drown and die as she had.

With this opening, there's no question magic is real. The villain is using weather magic to exact revenge.

Don't be fooled by the sheer number of examples that opening "the right way" with weather is easy to do. For every successful attempt, there are a thousand bad ones. My advice is to avoid a laundry list of weather descriptions and instead treat it like setting:[3] Make it a character by giving your hero an *emotional attachment* to it.

~

CHAPTER 10 FOOTNOTES

- [1] To be fair, "It was a dark and stormy night" is *not* the worst opening ever written, especially for the time (1830), but because most people *believe* it is, it becomes true for them and trust me, their "truth" can hurt you.
- [2] Like the "Anonymous Terrible Author" excerpts, uncredited ones like these are written by me to illustrate my point.
- [3] See Story Secret #7: "Make Your Setting A Character" in Chapter 7: Premonition.

III

MEMOIR

STORY HOOKS FOR NONFICTION

*Learn how to share your life story with the same raw passion
as your favorite celebrity, entrepreneur, or icon*

WRITING A DYNAMITE MEMOIR

HOW TO HOOK READERS WITH YOUR LIFE STORY

MEMOIR DIFFERS from autobiography because it focuses on moments and events rather than a whole life. As such, it is the most fiction-like of nonfiction and a genre unto itself.

Most memoirs use monologue to hook readers, so that's what I'm going to focus on. You'll notice, however, that mystery is frequently combined with monologue, and to surprisingly strong effect. If you'd like to explore starting your memoir with one of the other successful ways to open, I've included ideas for each at the end of this chapter.

Like fiction, it's often easiest to hook readers with trouble:

Two days compete for the worst day of my life: The first day is the day I was taken from my mother; the second is the day I arrived at the Mosses' foster home four years later.

— ASHLEY RHODES-COURTER, THREE LITTLE WORDS

You can't get simpler than that. We instantly know the author had a bad childhood. How bad remains to be seen...

Some of the most shocking memoirs hook us with sex, crime, addiction or violence:

In the darkness, he touches me, his long, strong fingers moving across the surface of my skin, his breath hot and real near my ear. He kisses me tenderly, my ear, my neck, my mouth. Slides my shirt over my head, the movement choreographed with his breath. Then his fingers on the button of my jeans, the hesitation. *Will she let me do this?* he must be wondering. And my wordless answer, a movement of the hips. *Yes, yes, always yes.*

— KERRY COHEN, LOOSE GIRL: A MEMOIR OF
PROMISCUITY

Remember when I said you can't open with full-on sex? That's still true, but that's not what Cohen is doing. She's giving a *brief* erotic memory filled with insight into her younger self. And after that paragraph, we return to her in the present reflecting on that scene and how it impacted her life.

You could do the same thing by teasing action, mystery, or any of the other ten ways instead—as long as it's exciting. Be careful not to go too long or you may end up with what amounts to a problem prologue.

You can open with addiction:

It's maybe twelve-thirty at night. I am high on OxyContin.

— AMY DRESNER, MY FAIR JUNKIE

You can open with shame and abuse:

When I was ten, my father changed me forever.

— BARBARA AMAYA, NOBODY'S GIRL

You can open with war:

It was the end of May, 1944. We had been in England eight months while others fought, and now our time had come. A last inspection, a last short-arm; clean the barracks and police the area. Every man gets a new jumpsuit and an orange smoke grenade. We move out at noon.

— DAVID KENYON WEBSTER, PARACHUTE INFANTRY

You can open with a quest for justice:

That summer I hunted the serial killer at night from my daughter's playroom. For the most part I mimicked the bedtime routine of a normal person. Teeth brushed. Pajamas on. But after my husband and daughter fell asleep, I'd retreat to my makeshift workspace and boot up my laptop, that fifteen-inch-wide hatch of endless possibilities.

— MICHELLE MCNAMARA, I'LL BE GONE IN THE DARK

Here's a more subtle example of memoir from a book that spent seven years on *The New York Times* bestseller list, and is a classic of its kind:

I was sitting in a taxi, wondering if I had overdressed for the evening, when I looked out the window and saw Mom rooting through a dumpster.

— JEANETTE WALLS, THE GLASS CASTLE

Wow! What's going on here? In just one sentence, the author has hooked us. She does this by introducing the hero first, then saving the problem (her Mom) for last.

CELEBRITY MEMOIRS

Maybe you're famous, or know someone who is. Celebrities are almost always interesting to read about, especially to their fans. But just because people buy the book based on their fame, that doesn't mean you don't have to hook them right from the start.

Here's how Grammy winner Phil Collins does it in his memoir, *Not Dead Yet*:

> I can't hear a thing.
>
> Much as I try to shake free the blockage, my right ear is unyielding. I attempt a little rummage with a cotton swab. I know this is never advised—the eardrum is sensitive, especially if it's been subject to a lifetime of drumming.
>
> But I'm desperate. My right ear is kaput. And it's my *good* ear, my left having been dicky for a decade. Is this it? Has music, at last, done me in? Am I finally deaf?
>
> — PHIL COLLINS, NOT DEAD YET

This isn't fancy prose, but memoir doesn't need to be. Above all else, it needs to be heartfelt, to put you inside the head of the author.

What could be more terrifying to a musician than going deaf? What about going deaf right before he's about to go back onstage and perform for the first time in years? Well, that's exactly what happened to Phil, and he writes about it painfully, honestly. That's all you need to do.

If you want to clean it up later, or hire a ghostwriter to dress it up for you, you can. But the most important thing is to get the words down—words dripping with emotion.

Here's another example of a celebrity musician memoir, this time punk and metal legend, Lita Ford:

> I guess I could start with when I was born or my first concert or the first time I picked up a guitar or something like that. We'll get there. But if you want to know the moment when everything started to shift for me, it was my sixteenth birthday party.
>
> — LITA FORD, LIVING LIKE A RUNAWAY

Like Phil Collins, this is simple prose, but effective. Lita is making us a promise, and that promise is yeah, she's going to give us the big picture, but she's also not going to waste our time with anything that isn't important. She's going to jump right to the main event, that catalyst moment that led her on the rocky path to stardom.

Let's compare Lita's memoir of being in The Runaways with that of her bandmate, Cherie Curie:

> My twin sister, Marie, and I looked uncharacteristically plain that night. In fact, we looked like any pair of normal fifteen-year-old girls from the Valley. A pair of blue jeans, our plainest, most boring blouse. No makeup, no nothing, but the "plain Jane" look was deliberate. Tonight was a special night, and the outfits carefully chosen.
>
> — CHERIE CURIE, NEON ANGEL

Carefully chosen for what? Obviously, Cherie and her twin are up to something, and it's probably no good...

Which opening do you like better? Which hooks you harder, faster? Which is the way you would write the biggest moment of your life?

Finally, I'm going to leave you with the opening to Pat Benatar's memoir. This is also simply written, but takes off like a rocket.

> I was never just a girl's girl. I grew up wanting to do boy things. Nail polish and baby dolls weren't enough for me. I wanted to be making a fort or climbing a tree. Boys seemed to have all the fun. They got to use a hammer and nails. They got to sneak into abandoned houses and go exploring. They were out riding go-karts. All that was right up my alley.
>
> And the boys I hung around with made me tough. At first they were merciless—they never cut me any slack. You want to be on the baseball team? Use this thin mitt that hurts your hands so badly you have to bite your cheek not to cry. You want to hang out in our clubhouse? Get ready to have earthworms squished onto your bare

legs. It was trial by fire, but in the end, I wouldn't have been caught dead crying over a skinned knee. All this made me fierce, and soon they realized that I was "okay for a girl," which was just fine with me, because I had a plan.

— PAT BENATAR, BETWEEN A HEART AND A ROCK PLACE

Simple works. What was Pat's plan, and how did it change her life? If you're not hooked, you might as well be dead. In fact, check your pulse right now, because I'm pretty sure you are!

Even if you're not famous, that doesn't mean you can't learn from celebrity memoirs. Maybe you played in a bunch of garage bands that went nowhere. That's fine too. In some ways, it's even more interesting—if you have the right kind of stories, and you tell them in the right order, with the right story hook.

I know I used all musician examples, but honestly, your profession doesn't matter. You could be a doctor, lawyer, businessman, politician, housewife, soldier, criminal—*anyone*—and still benefit from opening your memoir in a similar manner.

The real question is: *Do you have an interesting story to tell?* Will it interest large numbers of people who don't know you and have never heard of you? Then by all means, tell it!

MARKET REALITIES

If you're not famous, you're going to need a bigger hook than if you're a celebrity. How do you stand out? Find a gimmick, an angle. Did you know somebody famous? Were you present at some famous event? Write about your life in relation to that!

If none of those apply, is there a local or regional angle to exploit? Or maybe an issue that affects lots of people, like substance abuse, child abuse, abusive relationships, disability, mental illness, crime, family... some kind of struggle people want to read about, and who *might* be willing to give your memoir a chance to help them understand their own experience.

Whatever your angle, attach it to a universal theme, like "be careful what you wish for" or "money can't buy happiness" to help catch reader interest.

Two questions you need to answer before writing your memoir:

1. *Why are writing it?*
2. *Who is your target audience?*

Be as specific as possible; no book is for "everybody," and if you try to please everyone, you'll please no one.

Being an author can turn you into a highly-sought after and well-paid expert on your subject. Experts who are also authors find it easier to get media coverage and interviews. Worst case scenario, you ought to be able to get a speaking slot at your local library, church, or an interview in your local newspaper or radio talk show. Best case scenario? The sky's the limit!

- If your memoir is about your experience in an industry, you could parlay that into writing about your industry in general, even interviewing others in it, teaching it, etc.
- If you are an entrepreneur, your goal may be not to sell a ton of books but to get clients for your business—especially if you charge a lot of money for your products and/or services. A book is a *low cost entry point* to get customers into your sales funnel. So your book would include calls to action to visit your website, join your mailing list, etc.
- If you are a speaker, your goal is to get more speaking gigs and command higher fees. Being an author makes you far more likely to be booked *and* gives you something to sell at your engagements. Think about it: Who would you rather have speak at your event: some random nobody or the author of a book on whatever topic your company or organization is interested in?

HOW TO OPEN A MEMOIR WITHOUT MONOLOGUE

I'm going to close with one last thought, because I know it's something I would be wondering if I was writing my memoir.

What if you don't want to hook readers with monologue? After all, there are a lot of other cool ways to hook readers described in this book. Could you use one of them instead?

The answer is yes! Of course, but certain types of memoirs lend themselves better to different hooks. I'll go over them quickly now so you'll be able to narrow down your list:

- Were you in a war or riot? Were you assaulted? Did you play sports? Action could be your hook, such as impressions of fast, violent motion, then pulling back to reveal you in it.
- What was the one thing someone told you that inspired you to become who you are today? Use that dialogue as your hook.
- The profound statement is a good hook if you're a poet, teacher, philosopher, academic, or entrepreneur. Use the statement as a shortcut to the theme of your memoir, or as a metaphor for your life.
- Did something great or terrible happen to you? Foreshadow that great or terrible thing with a premonition or profound statement.
- Were you involved in some great mystery? Then Mystery might be your hook.
- Does your memoir take place in an exotic or unique location or during a natural disaster? Does the location play an influential role in your memoir? Hook with setting or weather.
- Were you involved with a villain? Were *you* the villain? Or were you the victim? Hook with that. Note that I use "victim" here purely for its alliterative value; replace it with "survivor" if you find that word more accurate and empowering.

AFTERWORD

THIS PART OF THE OMNIBUS may be over, but your adventure has just begun! The difference is now you're armed, armored, and ready to kick some ass. As you write your book, remember:

There are no blank pages, only possibilities.

The path is clear. The secret formula is yours! Make sure you use it because no matter what kind of fiction you write, today's market demands you hook your reader from the first sentence.

Nobody is willing to wait for your story to "get good." It has to be good right from the start. Delaying even a few paragraphs is fatal. Your opening must be *exciting*. It must be *provocative*. And I know you can do it. Now get out there and write some books!

— JACKSON DEAN CHASE
www.JacksonDeanChase.com

P.S.: If you enjoyed this book, please leave a review to help others in their author journey.

WRITING HEROES & VILLAINS

A MASTERCLASS IN GENRE FICTION

PREFACE

WELCOME to *The Ultimate Author's Guide to Writing Heroes & Villains.* This edition collects the first three volumes of my bestselling *How to Write Realistic Fiction* series, including quick start guides on *How to Write Realistic Characters, How to Write Realistic Men,* and *How to Write Realistic Women.* For this "ultimate" edition, I have revised and expanded them all.

This book is jam-packed with the essentials of how to write compelling heroes, villains, love interests, sidekicks, and teams, all the way down to the entire supporting cast and even those wacky minor characters that add so much spice to scenes.

It includes how to write anti-heroes, reluctant heroes, and catalyst heroes, plus templates for the heroic "everyman," tricksters, warriors, and characters with special powers (whether psychic, superhero, or supernatural).

Not only do I cover all that hero business, but I cover villains too: tempters, traitors, false mentors, and the rest of the rogues gallery we love to hate.

I also go into incredible, eye-opening detail about how to write realistic male and female characters. If you've ever struggled to write the opposite sex, then this book is for you. Not just hair, fashion, and makeup tips, either (although they're in here too), but real in-depth gender psychology. You'll learn the secret "rules" by which men and women operate: how they think and *why* they act the way they do.

I've broken the subjects up into three easy to read parts to help you find the information you need fast:

- Part 1: *How to Write Realistic Characters*
- Part 2: *How to Write Realistic Men*
- Part 3: *How to Write Realistic Women*

This is a book for anyone serious about the craft of writing fiction, comics, or screenplays. I've condensed all my years of study and practice into one fun, easy book, loaded with examples from your favorite TV, films, comics, and novels.

Come on in and take the ride!

— JACKSON DEAN CHASE
Get a free book at
www.JacksonDeanChase.com

"...Nothing works if you don't have interesting characters and a good story to tell."

— HAROLD RAMIS

HOW TO WRITE REALISTIC CHARACTERS

INTRODUCTION

"Things were easier for the old novelists… their heroes were good through and through, their villains wholly bad."

— W. SOMERSET MAUGHAM

TODAY'S READERS want complex, realistic characters that struggle as much as they succeed. I'm not just talking about external struggles, but internal ones. Characters can't be too good or too evil, but must possess some shades of gray. In short, they should seem real—and real people are flawed.

What about carefully constructed plots and world-building? Are having these enough to make up for a lack of realistic characters? No. All your plots and setting details won't mean a thing if readers don't care about your characters.

That's where this book comes in. By implementing the strategies you learn in this quick start guide, you will have an unbeatable system for creating the compelling characters your story deserves.

— JACKSON DEAN CHASE
Get a free book at www.JacksonDeanChase.com

THE DIFFERENCE BETWEEN PERFECT AND REALISTIC CHARACTERS

"Perfect heroines, like perfect heroes, aren't relatable, and if you can't put yourself in the protagonist's shoes, not only will they not inspire you, but the book will be pretty boring."

— CASSANDRA CLARE

EVERY HERO SHOULD BE LIKABLE in some way, or at least interesting. To do that, your hero needs to display some measure of wit and charm, as well as enough willpower to stand up to the villain. But heroes can't be perfect. They must be flawed, or risk becoming boring. That's the difference between Batman and Superman.

Batman's got all kinds of flaws, Superman's perfect. Which one sells more copies and puts more butts in seats? Batman. You can't fix perfect. It will always ring false to give Superman issues after he's already been established as perfect (and perfectly boring) for decades. Now if Batman overcomes a flaw, fans will be proud of him, but they won't get bored because they know he'll never be perfect, no matter how hard he tries.

Blowing up the Death Star or teaching an uptight town how to dance are all well and good. This outer journey is the main plot, the story arc that changes the world (or some small part of it). It's also the initial reason people buy into your story, but it's not what truly satisfies them. What they really want to see are heroes who struggle to change themselves in relation to their outer journey.

To do this, every hero needs an inner journey. They get one by facing down their flaws—this constitutes the character arc which makes up the emotional subplot. The success or failure of the character arc sets the tone for the story arc. Let me say that again:

The success or failure of the character arc sets the tone for the story arc.

It's the difference between the bittersweet tragedy of *Butch Cassidy and the Sundance Kid* and the joyful triumph of *Star Wars, Episode IV: A New Hope*. Butch and Sundance struggle to change and fail, so they must die (albeit in a blaze of glory). Luke Skywalker and Han Solo struggle to change and succeed, so they live and triumph and go on to have other adventures in a galaxy far, far away.

Note that "live or die" can simply mean "win or lose." Some losers get a second chance in the sequel. For example, Rocky Balboa loses the big boxing match to Apollo Creed at the end of *Rocky*, but beats him in *Rocky II*, and guess what? It's twice as satisfying for Rocky and the audience. If Rocky had failed to beat Creed a second time, the audience would have been justifiably angry at both Rocky and the screenwriter. The whole sequel would have been pointless!

That's not to say that you can't have a chronic "loser" continue his adventures (see The Catalyst Hero, below), but he must be a true underdog people can root for. And because he rarely changes (or needs to), that means he must change the lives of those he comes into contact with for the better. He helps others succeed at their story and character arcs, but ends up alone and riding off into the sunset at the end (as in *Mad Max: Fury Road*).

Eventually, this type of hero must complete his overarching story and character arc, and he should do so successfully. After all, he's suffered so long, he deserves it and the audience demands it. In most cases, this ends the series, so if you're not ready to end it, you should give your underdog glimmers of hope every so often instead—both to remind him and the audience what's at stake in the bigger picture.

While it's generally accepted wisdom that when the hero's inner journey fails, the outer one does too (and vice versa), that's not always the case. There are exceptions where succeeding at an inner journey could mean the hero no longer cares to succeed on his outer journey.

For example, consider the tough jock who passes his prom king crown to the lonely outcast because it means more to the outcast than it ever will to him. He's learned this the hard way over the course of the story, overcoming his arrogant jock flaws in the process. So by the end, he's not only willing to sacrifice outer success for inner success, he *must* do it, or he won't be able to live with himself.

The jock has changed and grown as a person, and so his original outer journey no longer holds meaning to him—but helping the outcast does, and that becomes his new one. The best part is this helps the outcast complete his inner and outer journey as well. The outcast no longer can fail to hide behind excuses of "nobody likes me" and "all jocks are jerks." If you've done your job right, and written the jock and outcast as realistic, flawed characters who we can empathize with, then you've written a winner.

A BRIEF OVERVIEW OF THREE-ACT STRUCTURE

"I believe in three-act structure. When I say that to novel people, or people in the world of books, they go, 'Well, that's a film thing.' However, even a good joke has three acts."

— STEPHEN J. CANNELL

THE HERO'S STORY and character arc can be broken down into a simple Three-Act Structure:

In Act 1, the hero is briefly seen living in her Ordinary World, and we learn she has a problem that needs fixing. This problem is usually invisible to the hero and must be pointed out by a member of the supporting cast, or sometimes a minor character. The hero does not know how to change at this point.

Regardless, an inciting incident (aka "the catalyst") occurs that forces the hero out of her Ordinary World. This could be a zombie invasion, losing her job, getting cancer, etc. The villain easily defeats her, but she stubbornly clings to the "safety" of her Ordinary World, not realizing the harder she fights, the more trouble she gets into.

Basically, as a writer, you need to keep asking yourself, "How can I make things worse for my hero?" That's what pushes her toward change, and also what determines the pace of the story. Too fast, and there is *not enough time* for her to properly reflect on changing. That will make the change feel forced and not credible. Too slow, and there is *too much time* for her to reflect and second-guess. Her change will seem snail-like and your story becomes boring.

In Act 2, the hero takes defensive actions to evade the villain until she reaches her breaking point. She must be made to see and confront that who she was is no longer who she is or wants to be. There is no turning back. She is becoming a new person now, with new skills, new allies, and new goals, but she is not all the way there yet.

This realization only happens *after* the villain attacks her and her allies harder than ever and she is defeated again. This signals the mid-point of the story. The hero emerges determined to change and grow into a person capable of defeating the villain.

(Note that in more literary, character-driven works, the "villain" could be addiction, mental illness, or some other inner demon, though it will have villainous physical manifestations via police, coworkers, doctors, lawyers, etc.)

In Act 3, the hero goes on the offensive. However, even though she wins some fights, this does not vanquish the villain—it only shows how insanely powerful he is. The hero is again defeated, coming close to death herself and/or losing someone close to her (often a mentor who is killed or love interest who is captured). She has reached an all-time low and contemplates suicide, surrender, or escape.

The villain seems invincible. But what the hero does not realize is that the confrontation has given her a valuable insight into how the villain can be defeated. This insight is something that should have been previously foreshadowed in the story, though it would not have been known to the hero or deemed important if it was. The insight could take the shape of an ability, ally, object, or information.

Rather than give in to despair, the hero decides to confront the villain one last time. By doing so, she proves she is no longer becoming a hero, but has become one. This gives her the courage and confidence she needs to recognize the valuable insight and formulate a clever plan to surprise the villain. There is hope now—real, not imagined. She gathers her allies and weapons, and using the insight, attacks the villain with everything she's got!

The simplest stories would let this play out to a predictable (and boring) happy ending, but I'm betting you don't want to settle for that. What should happen instead is the insight the hero is relying on proves to be only half-right, not enough, or plain wrong—perhaps even a trick.

However, if the insight is completely correct, then the villain has set up some deadly (and unexpected) obstacle to prevent the hero from exploiting his weakness.

In any event, the villain, realizing the danger he is in, takes immediate action to surprise, demoralize, and defeat the hero with everything he has. The hero and villain both take heavy losses, including the defeat of their allies (in ascending order, from weakest to strongest). But it's still not enough to stop the villain. It's time for the final showdown, the climax where the hero and villain face each other, one on one.

It is at this point the villain can't resist saying or doing something so gloating or hateful that it forces the hero to instantly resolve her inner journey one way or another.

If she fails to resolve her inner journey, the villain soundly defeats her and we have a tragic ending.

If she succeeds, she suddenly realizes what she must do—she must sacrifice (or be willing to sacrifice) everything she holds dear, including her own life, to defeat the villain. If the valuable insight to the villain's defeat was only half-right before, the other half falls into place now, and the hero is quick to act on it.

In his arrogance, the villain is unprepared or unwilling to believe the hero could ever beat him, and though he makes a last-ditch attempt to stop her, he cannot withstand her relentless, inspired assault. The villain is soundly defeated, the day is won, and the hero enjoys her happy ending.

That does not mean the villain (or the evil he represents) is gone forever, but it will take time for to rebuild, and the hero will be better prepared to fight next time.

This type of last minute "pop-up scare" or epilogue is common in horror stories, but can be relied upon whenever you have need of a strong, recurring villain or greater evil.

HERO ARCHETYPES

"In the film world, we can all be heroes. In the real world, where heroism can cost you your life or the life of the ones you love, people aren't so willing to make those sacrifices. When they do, they are set apart from the rest of us."

— JOHN RHYS-DAVIES

THERE ARE TWO MAIN HERO ARCHETYPES: Catalyst Heroes and Reluctant Heroes. Both offer their own set of challenges and rewards. Note that rival theories suggest there are at least eight, and as many as fifty-two archetypes. To me, that's not just confusing, it's overwhelming. What I've done is condense all that fancy talk down into the two main archetypes and six subtypes you find in popular novels, short stories, comic books, and screenplays. Rest assured, all of the fifty-two archetypes from other theories easily fit into my "bite-size" formula.

The Catalyst Hero comes into your story fully formed. His role is not to change (well, not too much or too often), but rather to enact positive change in others. Series heroes are often catalysts. Think Captain America, James Bond, The Lone Ranger, or most any action hero. They are fearless, self-sacrificing exemplars of their type who rarely make mistakes they can't scheme or fight their way out of.

Most catalyst heroes are respected and rewarded for doing good deeds, but not all. Some catalysts are deeply mistrusted and misunderstood, even persecuted and pursued (such as Kane in *Kung-Fu*, David Banner in *The Incredible Hulk*, or Richard Kimble in *The Fugitive*, which are pretty much all the same brilliant TV series).

Even if your catalyst hero is retired and presents himself as a reluctant hero, deep down, he's not. That's because of the speed with which he transitions back to his old heroic ways. He's already made the journey, and being a hero to him is just like riding a bicycle: he never forgot how to do it.

The benefit of the retired catalyst is you get to flirt with the reluctant hero tropes without having to do all the work. The retired catalyst's catch phrase is, "I'm getting too old for this," and maybe he grumbles a lot, but he's secretly pleased to be recognized and needed again. Retirement doesn't suit him, and he'd rather go out in a blaze of glory.

Reluctant Heroes come into the story unwilling at first to take heroic action. Some may arrive already successful at one thing or another, while others will be unformed nobodies or even malformed minor villains. They may begin complacent, ignorant, naïve, arrogant, or selfish, but never irredeemably bad or broken. Think Frodo Baggins, Han Solo, Spider-Man, and Tyrion Lannister from *Game of Thrones*. None of them *wanted* to be heroes, but circumstances forced them to be… even if they went kicking and screaming (or drunk).

Reluctant heroes are punished for doing good deeds. All it takes is one spontaneous act of kindness or mercy to strip them of everything and change their destiny forever. This is especially true for minor villains who undergo a change of heart. They end up paying an unthinkable price for doing the right thing because they hang out with bigger villains who regard kindness as not only a weakness, but dangerous in their line of work.

The rewards reluctant heroes get for their deeds are small and personal at first. As they grow into full-fledged heroes (stumbling along the way), the rewards get bigger, but so do the risks.

Reluctant heroes can be the most satisfying to write and to watch, because they have an inner journey as well as an outer one. We see them change themselves for the better even as they enact positive change in others.

HERO SUBTYPES

"Heroes are ordinary people who make themselves extraordinary."

— GERARD WAY

THERE ARE SIX COMMON SUBTYPES OF HEROES: Three mundane (everyman, trickster, and warrior), and three special (psychic, superhero, and supernatural). The three specials are really just templates you layer over mundanes to give them more exciting powers. Each has different strengths and flaws.

EVERYMAN HERO

The Everyman (or Everywoman) is neither amazingly fast nor strong, and has no special powers. What he does have is a core set of beliefs and willingness to stand up to threats. He uses these (and an awful lot of willpower) to win the day. An everyman may also have a specialized skill set that helps him overcome problems, or simply a big heart and an open mind. He could be a nobody or somebody in his world: from privileged elite to the working class or even homeless.

The fragility of this hero often confines him to YA fiction, romance novels, dramas, horror, legal or medical thrillers, and more literary stories where he is not expected to confront (or survive) the sort of world-shattering villains Trickster, Warrior, and Special heroes must face.

That doesn't mean an everyman doesn't lead an interesting life or can't change the world—he just does it in a way that makes sense for him, and is commensurate with his position and abilities.

However, some Everyman heroes grow into Tricksters, Warriors, and/or Specials, usually via an origin story where they begin without any powers and slowly develop them over the course of the story. Occasionally, you will see this concept reversed, such as Superman learning to hide his powers to fit in as an alien living among humans.

EVERYMAN EXAMPLES: Ben Mears from *'Salem's Lot*, Karl Kolchak from *The Night Stalker*, Elizabeth Bennett from *Pride and Prejudice*, Frodo Baggins from *The Lord of the Rings*, Dr. Leonard "Bones" McCoy from *Star Trek*, and Vikka Raymer from my sci-fi action/thriller, *Drone*.

TRICKSTER HERO

Tricksters are fast and clever, but never as physically powerful as warriors. They rely on their wits and flexibility to win the day, which may cause them to underestimate warriors. Most wizards, thieves, spies, and businessmen fall into this category.

TRICKSTER EXAMPLES: Doctor Who, Sherlock Holmes, Captain Picard from *Star Trek: The Next Generation*, Gandalf and Legolas from *The Lord of the Rings*, Danny Ocean from *Ocean's Eleven*, Mr. Spock from *Star Trek*, Peter Quill ("Starlord") from *Guardians of the Galaxy*, and Jon Warlock from my urban fantasy thriller, *Warlock Rising*.

WARRIOR HERO

Warriors are physically powerful and/or strategic, but never as fast or clever as tricksters. They rely on brute force and sound tactics to win the day, which may cause them to underestimate tricksters.

WARRIOR EXAMPLES: Captain Kirk from *Star Trek*, Conan the Barbarian, John McClane from *Die Hard*, Gimli from *The Lord of the Rings*, Mack Bolan, The Punisher, and Andrus Eaves from my urban fantasy thriller, *Titan* (co-written with Daniel Mignault).

IMPORTANT

Both warriors and tricksters will often have one or more signature weapons, tactics, or ruses they favor, and that fans of the character will expect to see them use *at least once* per story. To prevent this from getting old, you should mix things up a bit, and follow a progression, if possible.

For example, in my bestselling *Beyond the Dome* science fiction series, Rylee Mersum is a spy and assassin with a cybernetic arm. Over the course of three books, we see her use her "robot arm" in new and exciting ways. In *Warrior*, she shows the arm has a retractable sword blade in it. She uses it to punch through metal and kill her enemies. In *Elite*, she reveals she can fire the sword blade to impale a target. In *Human*, she fires the sword blade to impale two targets attacking her down a narrow corridor. She also reveals she can detach the robot arm and control it via a neural implant in her skull.

With each new book, Rylee uses her robot arm in expected and unexpected ways. Because she is a paranoid, secretive anti-hero, she does not reveal to the rest of her team what all her abilities are the first time we meet her.

If Rylee had revealed more than one or two new uses for her robot arm in a single book, it would have seemed like I was cheating. So be careful what abilities you give your characters and how quickly you reveal them, but whatever you do, don't overdo it! Less is more.

BACKGROUND QUESTIONS

Regardless of whether your hero is an everyman, trickster, or warrior, you need to ask yourself the following questions about his background:

1. Why and where did your hero undergo his training?
2. Is he self-taught? If not, who was his mentor, and what is their relationship?
3. Did your hero undergo his training by choice, or was he forced to do it?
4. Does your hero work as a lone wolf, with a small team, as part of a larger organization he believes in, or is he on the run?

MUNDANE FLAWS

Being overly ambitious, arrogant, cowardly, disloyal or loyal (to the wrong people), driven, foolhardy, greedy, sarcastic, or selfish. Mundane heroes may be introverts or extroverts depending on their nature (for example, many computer hackers are introverts).

WARNING

Be careful creating hybrid trickster/warrior heroes. *A hero who is good at too many things is not only boring, but hard to find credible challenges for.* Which is not to say it can't be done, but you must give hybrid heroes extra flaws to make up for their extra strengths—not just one incredibly rare and stupid thing like kryptonite. For that reason, it may be better to create a hybrid everyman with a trickster or warrior. You can also do this by creating a hybrid of an everyman and one of the special subtypes below.

The superhero and urban fantasy genres excel at these hybrids, such as Spider-Man really being newspaper photographer, Peter Parker, and *True Blood* bar owner, Sam Merlotte, also being a shapeshifter. These characters may travel to other dimensions, but they live in the real world, including holding down real jobs and having the same annoying problems regular people do.

Sometimes, a better solution than a hybrid is to have your hero team up with his opposite. This not only replaces the need for your hero to excel in too many areas, but creates a ton of extra fun arising from their daily banter.

For example, in Fritz Lieber's fantasy classic, *Ill Met in Lankhmar*, Fafhrd (a sword-swinging warrior) teams up with the Gray Mouser (a thief and wizard trickster). Their strengths and weaknesses complement each other, allowing them to achieve things neither could on their own.

THE SPECIAL HERO (PSYCHIC, SUPERNATURAL, OR SUPERHERO TEMPLATES)

There must be some kind of backstory to explain your hero's powers, and you must also come up with a set of "rules" for what she can and can't do. Once you've set the rules in place, don't break them!

You might be able to *bend* the rules once or twice, but only with a clear, logical reason and only if there are extreme consequences for the hero as a result. It's also best if the situation cannot be repeated, otherwise readers will wonder why the hero just doesn't do it again.

Are your hero's special powers the result of a curse, gift, magical training, or mutation? Is it hereditary?

1. Is she self-taught (or even aware of her power)?
2. What kind of mentor taught (or will teach) her to embrace and develop her power? Then ask yourself:
3. Is the mentor human? If not, what is it and why is it here?
4. What are the mentor's ultimate goals, and is your hero aware or approving of them?
5. Does the mentor work alone, with a small team, or with a larger organization?
6. What is your hero's relationship like with her mentor?

PSYCHIC ABILITIES

Determine what type of abilities your hero has and if any other abilities exist in your world. Psychic Ability examples include:

- Empathy (reading emotions)
- Mediumship (communicating with spirits)
- Mind control
- Precognition (predicting the future)
- Psychometry (seeing the past by "reading" objects)
- Psychokinesis (aka telekinesis, moving objects)
- Pyrokinesis (creating/manipulating fire)
- Telepathy (mental communication, either one-way or two-way)

A psychic with more than one power should be better at one than the others, and her reliance on it should shape her personality and actions.

Because they live so much in their heads, psychics are often tricksters and introverts.

Examples: Allison Dubois from *Medium*, Sookie Stackhouse from *True Blood*, Lorraine Warren from *The Conjuring*, Professor Xavier from *X-Men*.

PSYCHIC FLAWS

Psychic powers are notoriously unreliable and not always accurate or able to be interpreted correctly. They may cause temporary or permanent mental or physical problems, as well as social issues. Some will not believe in the hero's gift, thus putting themselves (and potentially others) in danger when they fail to heed her warnings.

SUPERHEROES

Determine what type of superpower(s) your hero has, and what other kinds of powers (including the heroes and villains who use them) exist in your world.

1. Are superpowers regulated by the government?
2. Who knows his secret?
3. What happens if his secret identity is "outed"?
4. What civil and legal repercussions might he face?
5. Does the hero believe he has been chosen or otherwise gifted, or does he consider his powers a curse?
6. Does he believe he is superior to mundanes?

Super power examples include:

- Aquatic powers (Aquaman, Namor the Submariner)
- Armored bones or skin (Colossus, Wolverine)
- Animal powers (including claws, fangs, tail, wings)
- Energy projection (Cyclops, The Human Torch)
- Echolocation (Daredevil)
- Flight (without wings) (Superman)
- Immunity to energy weapons
- Immunity to mundane weapons (Superman)
- Invisibility (The Invisible Woman)
- Magnetism (Magneto)
- Mind control (Kilgrave from *Jessica Jones*)
- Shape- or size-shifting (Ant-Man, Mr. Fantastic)
- Superior intellect (Professor X)
- Superior senses (Spider-Man)
- Superior technology (Batman, Iron Man)
- Super strength (Superman, the Hulk, the Thing)
- Super speed (The Flash)
- Teleportation (Nightcrawler)

A superhero with more than one power should be better at one more than the rest, and his reliance on his "signature power" should shape his personality and actions.

Superheroes can be tricksters or warriors based on their powers. They may be introverts or extroverts. It could fun to play against type (a "Mind Master" who hates people).

SUPERHERO FLAWS

The most obvious is having a secret identity that imperils the hero and loved ones if revealed, or perhaps the powers are useless in certain situations (for example, Superman in the presence of kryptonite, or Green Lantern having no power over anything colored yellow), or else the hero's quest to help others forces him to miss out on opportunities to help himself (such as Spider-Man).

SUPERNATURAL HEROES

Determine what type of supernatural creature or character your hero is and/or what type of magic they know (if any), and what other kinds of creatures and/or magic exist in your world.

Common examples include:

- Corporeal Undead (vampires, zombies, etc.)
- Spirits (Angels, Demons, Djinni, Faeries, Ghosts)
- Shape-shifters (werewolves, etc.)
- Witches, Wizards, and other spellcasters

Magic examples include:

- Abjuration (protection magic)
- Conjuration (banishing/summoning creatures/objects)
- Divination (obtaining knowledge through magical means, including scrying)

- Evocation (summoning and projecting lethal types of energy to destroy objects or enemies)
- Mind Magic (curses, illusion, mind control)
- Nature (elemental energy, communication with plants and animals, healing, weather control)
- Necromancy (destroying or transferring spiritual or physical energy from one person or object to another, speaking to spirits, and raising the dead back to life or as undead)
- Transmutation/Enchantment (changing creatures or objects into another type or adding new abilities to them, either temporarily or permanently, including creating magic items)

Spellcasters may be well-rounded wizards who who know a bit of everything, while others may specialize in mastering a few specific types or subtypes of magic, such as ice witches, shape-shifters, or necromancers.

In some worlds, it may be impossible for casters of one type of magic to use an opposing type, such as fire and ice magic, or nature and necromancy. It may be easier to learn complementary types of magic, such as wind and water magic to help them sail and defeat enemy ships. Perhaps some casters pride themselves on unusual or "forbidden" combinations of magic, such as a necromancer who masters nature magic to heal both the living and undead.

Supernatural heroes can be tricksters or warriors based on their powers and how they use them. Most are introverts who avoid contact with mundanes. With their own kind (or those they trust) they may feel free to act as extroverts.

Examples: Dr. Strange, Gandalf, John Constantine, Damon and Stefan Salvatore from *The Vampire Diaries.*

SUPERNATURAL FLAWS

Perhaps the hero's supernatural powers are only available under certain conditions, or have built-in strengths and weaknesses that limit the hero's effectiveness in specific situations (such as a vampire being strong at night and powerless in daylight), or else her powers are unpredictable (like chaos magic), or come at a high price—for example, reducing her sanity or lifespan with each use, or making her less and less human.

OVERCOMING FLAWS

Since all special heroes wield dangerous, mysterious powers, they should practice to gain mastery of them, and carefully consider the cost to themselves and to others before using them—or Very Bad Things will happen!

ANTI-HEROES

"I'm not sure why I'm so drawn to heroes who do bad things and to villains who think they're the good guys, but I do find that moral ambiguity and conflict makes for great characters."

— BARRY EISLER

IF A CHARACTER DOES UNLIKEABLE THINGS for good reasons, then he's an anti-hero. Humanize him wherever and whenever possible; make us understand why he does what he does the way he that he does it. Make sure the people he is up against are even more ruthless and cruel so your anti-hero looks good by comparison.

A great example of this is Clint Eastwood's "Man with No Name" in *A Fistful of Dollars*, *For a Few Dollars More*, and *The Good, the Bad, and the Ugly*. Clint's character is a greedy opportunist, but the people he goes up against are even worse.

What makes the "Man with No Name" likable is that he has traits his opponents lack: a sense of humor and moral compass that keep him from ever having to hate himself. There are certain things he won't do, even if it prevents him from reaching his goal. This keeps the "Man with No Name" from becoming a true villain, no matter what crimes he commits. Despite his flaws, he still has a heart, and we love him for it.

We see this type of character time and time again in classic *noir* and crime capers. More recent examples include Johnny Depp's portrayal of "Captain Jack Sparrow" in *Pirates of the Carribbean*, and Billy Bob Thornton's hit man, "Lorne Malvo," in the first season of the *Fargo* TV series.

VILLAINS AND TEMPTERS

"There is a charm about the forbidden that makes it unspeakably desirable."

— MARK TWAIN

WHEN WRITING VILLAINS, the key concept to remember is that the villain believes he is the hero of his own story. He is not there to twirl his mustache and laugh while doing "Very Bad Things" for no discernible reason. That's not a credible villain, that's a cartoon character!

Villains should be the twisted mirror image of your hero. They are what your hero will become should they let their ego control them and surrender to temptation. That's why so many confrontations include some variation of the villain telling the hero, "We are the same, you and I. Only I am not afraid to get what I want."

Rather than just have a hero and villain oppose each other, more complex stories include a third type of character, the Tempter[1]. This character represents what the hero will become should he give in to the villain, and there is usually some backstory involved between the hero and tempter (often a friendly rivalry).

Unlike the villain, the tempter actually respects the hero, and wants to convert him to her side because she genuinely believes he will benefit from it.[2] She may even suggest that if the hero and tempter work together, they can take down the villain far easier than if the hero attempts to go it alone.

The problem is, the tempter often doesn't want to just defeat the villain, she wants to *replace* him. The tempter is guided by a misguided "higher purpose" that justifies her actions. She sincerely thinks she can do a better job than the villain—often in a less villainous way. She will be sincerely hurt when the hero rejects her plan, but will not let it stop her from going through with it.

Perhaps the most famous example is Darth Vader's speech to Luke Skywalker in *The Empire Strikes Back*: "Luke, you can destroy the Emperor. He has foreseen this. *It is your destiny!* Join me, and together we can rule the galaxy as father and son…"

Another great example (from another LucasFilm classic) is the amoral French archaeologist René Belloq, who tries to convince Indiana Jones to help him aid the Nazis for their mutual gain in *Raiders of the Lost Ark*: "All your life has been spent in pursuit of archaeological relics. Inside the Ark are treasures beyond your wildest aspirations. You want to see it opened as well as I. Indiana, we are simply passing through history. This, this *is* history."

The tempter may also exist in a more long-term, harder to resist role as a lover, best friend, or family member. We see this with *femme fatales* in *noir* movies, and corrupt but family-minded business tycoons like J.R. Ewing on *Dallas*.

Like your hero, villains and tempters must believe what they are doing is right, and that their actions are helping someone (even if it's only truly themselves). Unlike heroes, villains and tempters are willing to sacrifice everything to achieve their goals, rarely pulling back from the brink (and being resentful when forced to).

However, it's not enough to simply show your villain or tempter doing bad things. You must show her justifying her actions (either to herself or others), and reveal the emotional toll these nefarious actions are taking on her.

Note that all the hero archetypes and subtypes I describe are available to villains too. Even your supporting cast and minor characters can benefit from them.

FOR MORE IDEAS about writing villains, whether human, alien, machine, or monster, be sure to read my bestselling book, *Writing Monsters & Maniacs*. It has everything you need (including plot ideas) to bring your perfect villain to life.

Additionally, if you are writing post-apocalyptic action or survival horror, read my book, *Writing Apocalypse & Survival*. It will walk you through the stages of the apocalypse, zombie virus incubation stages, how law enforcement, prepper, and survivalist characters will act, and much more, including two complete plot templates for on the road or siege scenarios, and how to combine them.

And if you need help describing your villains, I have a full line of *Writers' Phrase Books*, each tackling a different genre.

CHAPTER 6 FOOTNOTES

1 Some writing gurus refer to the Tempter as the Contagonist (*Dramatica*) or Deflector (*My Story Can Beat Up Your Story*). I prefer to use "Tempter."

2 The difference between the tempter and the false mentor and traitor from the next chapter is that the tempter never tries to disguise he's in league with the villain (or even that he is a villain, or at least morally compromised).

The tempter does not rejoice when the hero suffers. Further, the tempter will make at least some sincere, good faith attempt to save the hero from the villain at least once because of the bond they share—but rarely in a way that would permanently mess up the tempter's relationship with the villain. Too much is riding on it.

7

FALSE MENTORS AND TRAITORS

"I'm a traitor, but I don't consider myself a traitor... There's no special magic [to deceiving people]. Confidence is what does it. Confidence, and a friendly relationship with the [target]. Rapport, where you smile and you make him think that you like him."

— ALDRICH AMES

SOMETIMES A VILLAIN PRESENTS himself to the hero as a false mentor, friend, or ally. Famous examples include Chancellor Palpatine to Anakin Skywalker in the *Star Wars* prequels, Saruman to Gandalf in *The Lord of the Rings*, etc.

The hero remains blind to the warning signs because she loves the villain, or values him for some other important reason. They have something in common that binds them together.[1]

Perhaps the hero thinks she can change the mentor by leading him back on the right path. This creates wonderful opportunities for conflict, and plenty of ways for the reader to get to know the villain far more intimately than they might were he not as present in the hero's daily life.

Despite the hero's best efforts, the villain cannot be changed, and when the hero tries too hard, the villain throws off his disguise and makes his true nature clear. The story then becomes the epic struggle between the hero and her former mentor/ally/friend.

CHAPTER 7 FOOTNOTE

1 Unlike the tempter from Chapter 6, the false mentor and traitor do not act out of love or loyalty to the hero. That does not mean they hate them, just that they only view the hero as a pawn in their scheme.

When their true nature is revealed, the false mentor or traitor will often make a *token effort* to retain the hero's loyalty before fleeing or attacking. However, this is done solely for their convenience, not out of friendship. As such, their words will be lacking sincerity and attempt to motivate the hero through negative appeals to ambition, fear, or greed—rarely to serve the tempter's misguided "higher purpose."

REDEEMING THE VILLAIN

"...I definitely need to understand the villains I play. The best cause pain to anesthetize themselves against their own pain."

— RON PERLMAN

WHEN A GREATER EVIL than the villain himself is present, writers have another option: What if the villain realizes the true horror of what he has done? It is in this moment that one of three things can happen:

1. The hero seizes the moment to defeat the villain while he is distracted, then takes on the greater evil.
2. The greater evil destroys the villain, either from sensing the villain's wavering commitment, or from not caring about the villain at all.
3. Or, in the most satisfying version, the villain realizes the error of his ways and joins the hero to redeem himself.

Let's go into the third option with more detail. To redeem himself, the villain must be willing to sacrifice his plans (and usually his life) for the greater good. That does not mean the redeemed villain should win the final battle for the hero, merely that they should make it possible for the hero to win. The hero must still do the heavy lifting, or the ending becomes less satisfying. Not as bad as a *deus ex machina*, but still not quite right.

Let's look at *Return of the Jedi* for an example: During the final battle in the Death Star's throne room, Emperor Palpatine unleashes his Sith lightning to torture and kill Luke Skywalker. Darth Vader is overcome by guilt and remorse, and decides he cannot let his son perish anymore than he can continue to serve his diabolical master. Vader kills the Emperor to save Luke, *but that makes Vader the hero* when the original trilogy is supposed to be Luke's story, not Vader's (despite what any revisionist history the prequels might have imposed).

How much more satisfying would it have been were Vader to have sacrificed himself by wounding the Emperor so badly that Luke could have given Palpatine the final blow? It would have made Luke much cooler because then he would not only have saved his father from a life of evil, but killed the most awful tyrant the galaxy had ever seen.

SUPPORTING CHARACTERS

"Supporting characters are a great source to use to develop conflict within a story. In their own unique way each one of the supporting characters can create obstacles for the hero to overcome."

— VICTORIA LYNN SCHMIDT, 45 MASTER CHARACTERS

IT'S NEVER BEEN ENOUGH for writers to only develop their hero and villain. To create a truly memorable world that comes alive, nearly every character[1] in the book must have some character development. The amount depends on whether they are supporting cast or minor characters.

For example, Spider-Man has the best supporting cast in comic book history. Who can forget J. Jonah Jameson, Aunt May, Gwen Stacy, or Mary Jane Watson? Even some of his deadliest enemies are his friends when they're not under the influence of their demented alter-egos (Norman Osborn, aka the Green Goblin, or Dr. Curt Connors, aka the Lizard). Talk about conflict!

DEFINING THE SUPPORTING CAST

Your supporting cast includes the hero's love interest, best friend, mentor, and other primary allies—and sometimes rivals. These are the people your hero is willing to sacrifice herself for, and who would gladly sacrifice themselves for her cause. They need to be every bit as likable as your hero, perhaps even more so.

What would *Star Wars: Episode IV* be without Obi-Wan Kenobi, Han Solo, and Princess Leia? Inexperienced farm boy Luke Skywalker isn't interesting enough to carry the picture, let alone save the galaxy.

What about a less vanilla, more badass character like *Hellboy*? Sure, he could take on most enemies by himself, but how much more fun will his adventures be when Abe Sapien, Liz Sherman, and Johann Krauss are along for the ride? (The answer is a lot!)

A ton of other great supporting cast examples exist: Dr. Watson in *Sherlock Holmes*, Tonto in *The Lone Ranger*, etc. The reason these characters exist is to balance the hero, to give him gifts, training, and advice, and to move the story along while deepening it with bonds of love and friendship, romance and rivalry—and some much needed comedy relief and witty banter.

These characters don't even need to be your hero's friends—even disagreeable traveling companions can add a lot of fun. My favorite example is the bandit Tuco[2] (Eli Wallach) in *The Good, the Bad, and the Ugly*. Tuco is loud, stupid, and greedy, almost a cartoon character, yet without his presence, the film becomes too grim. By being such a jackass, Tuco makes both the hero (Clint Eastwood) look more heroic and the villain (Lee van Cleef) more villainous.

Even a lone wolf like James Bond has his Bond girls and supporting characters like Q and Moneypenny. They may not go with him on his adventures, but they put a face on the cause he's fighting for, and are a big part of what he has to look forward to between missions.

FOOTNOTES FOR CHAPTER 10

1 Obviously, you don't need to develop a random waitress who is just a "walk-on" with little to no dialogue or impact on your story, but don't overlook her either! Sometimes, these "walk-ons" can be expanded into making your scenes both more real *and* more memorable. See Chapter 14: Minor Characters for how to do it.

2 Normally, characters who refuse to change must die (literally or metaphorically) at the end of the story, but because Tuco is more jackass than true villain, and because the audience loves him, he gets to live. Whether or not Tuco uses this lucky break to mend his ways or seek revenge is left to the audience's imagination.

OPPOSITES ATTRACT

"Opposites create intense chemistry. There are more chances of fireworks when different people are together than similar personalities."

— SONAM KAPOOR

WHEN DESIGNING SUPPORTING CAST MEMBERS, keep in mind that they should complement each other as well as the hero:

- Being strong where the others are weak, and weak where the others are strong.
- They should be opposites in logic vs. emotion, courage vs. caution, love vs. hate, etc.
- They should have their own back stories, goals, and ambitions. And quirks. Plenty of quirks!
- They should each provide at least one idea that helps the hero and one that hinders him per story. The bigger the help or hindrance, the more readers will like them. That shows they are useful, but not suited to be the star of the show. That's your hero's job.

Perhaps the best example of this is the original *Star Trek* series. You have the brash, charming and ego-driven warrior, Captain Kirk, supported by calm, logical trickster Mr. Spock, and the curmudgeonly and cautious everyman, Dr. McCoy. They're all highly skilled, they all like each and respect each other, but they rarely agree on the best course of action. This makes for constant conflict, from light banter to actual fist fights! And that's what keeps people tuning in to watch them. It's not the genre or the special effects, *it's the characters*. Notice how the three mundane character subtypes are embodied here—you should strive to recreate this dynamic in any ensemble piece.

LOVE INTERESTS

"Immature love says: 'I love you because I need you.' Mature love says: 'I need you because I love you.'"

— ERICH FROMM

WHETHER HEROIC, villainous, or in-between, your hero's love interest should represent the hero's internal conflict—either what he is missing and seeking in his personal life, or his temptation not to change because her way is easier.[1] In this case, the hero must recognize she cannot be good for him in the long run and either decide to end it or succumb to temptation anyway.

By the same token, the hero must represent the same thing to the love interest: the hope for long-term change and wholeness, or the desperate clinging to bad habits in the name of short-term expediency and pleasure.

In stories without a romantic subplot, substitute a supporting character for the love interest and put them in a platonic relationship with your hero such as best friend, business partner, sibling, etc. Everything else remains the same, and this supporting character becomes the most important one in your hero's life, the one he cares about the most (even if he shouldn't).

If the hero fails on his inner journey, he will lose the love interest —often to death (with the hero to blame). However, the hero may also lose her to a rival or to her own ambitions. Due to the hero's bad decisions, she no longer sees him as compatible.

If the hero succeeds on his inner journey, the love interest becomes his personal reward on top of any external ones for accomplishing his outer journey.

IF YOU NEED HELP DESCRIBING romantic situations, grab a copy of my *Romance, Emotion, and Erotica Writers' Phrase Book*. It has thousands of ways to describe love, romance, and intimacy among humans, aliens, and monsters.

CHAPTER 11 FOOTNOTE

1 The *femme fatale* from *noir* is a classic example of this.

THE STAKES CHARACTER

"Being deeply loved by someone gives you strength, while loving someone deeply gives you courage."

— LAO TZU

THE VILLAIN IS HURTING PEOPLE, but you can't show them all or make us care even if you do. Enter the "stakes character." This is a single supporting character (usually a love interest, best friend, or sibling) who your hero loves deeply.

When the villain victimizes this character, the stakes are raised. Before, what the villain did may not have directly affected your hero, but this time, it's personal. Now the hero has no choice but to act. He will not rest until he rescues or avenges the stakes character.

Examples: Mary Jane Watson and Gwen Stacy from *Spider-Man*, Lois Lane and Jimmy Olsen from *Superman*, Uncle Owen and Aunt Beru from *Star Wars*.

Who is your stakes character and how far will the hero go to protect them?

One interesting idea is for the hero to lose the stakes character in stages, rather than all at once (such as from being kidnapped or killed). This will take a different emotional toll on the hero and create additional conflict. Some examples might include:

- The stakes character is jailed or sentenced to prison by the villain
- The stakes character is tempted, seduced, and/or corrupted by the villain
- The stakes character becomes mentally ill and is institutionalized by the villain
- The stakes character becomes physically ill and is hospitalized by the villain
- The stakes character is sent on a dangerous mission by the villain; this can be done knowingly if the stakes character is a soldier, bodyguard, or law enforcement; otherwise, the stakes character is unaware of the danger. In either case, they insist on going, and suffer a series of unfortunate events caused either by the villain or his enemies.

See how that changes things? Of course, these ideas can also be used for the hero as well, particularly if the villain is a false mentor or traitor (as described in chapter 7).

DESIGNING THE TEAM

"Once you declare your loyalty to a team, every person who doesn't support that team, it's their job to ruin you, to tell you you're an idiot and to tell you that you made the wrong choice."

— MARK HOPPUS

WHEN CREATING TEAMS OF ALLIES for your hero and villain, they should be mirror images of each other.[1] If the hero has a sidekick, the villain should as well, and that sidekick should complement the villain, just as the hero's sidekick complements him. By complement, I mean they have skills and powers the hero or villain lacks. This creates a more well-rounded team.

And that brings me to a book you absolutely need to read. It's one of my favorites, and it opened my eyes regarding how to create teams. It's called *My Story Can Beat Up Your Story* by Jeffrey Alan Shechter. In it, he states that beyond the hero or villain, there are certain archetypes on every team:

1. a Believer who loves and trusts in the hero and fills the role of sidekick, best friend, and/or love interest;

2. a Protector who embodies the hero or group's moral compass;
3. a Doubter who complains and questions everything;
4. a Feeler who reacts first and thinks later;
5. a Tempter who tries to pull the hero or villain off their path; and
6. a Thinker who analyzes everything before acting.

With smaller casts, some of these roles can played by the same character. In larger casts, you could have more than one of each, but try to make them different—one could be funny, the other serious.

Here are important questions to ask yourself about your teams:

1. Why did the characters join? Most will do so because they believe in the hero or villain's goals, or else supporting the team serves their own agenda (fame, fortune, love, loyalty, revenge, etc.).
2. Remember that only insane bad guys think of themselves as truly "evil" (and even then, only rarely), so give them a strong, logical motive to be on the villain's team. If they are connected to the villain through love, family, or friendship, even better.
3. Give each teammate at least one quirk to make them memorable, and then pay it off, like Indiana Jones being afraid of snakes in *Raiders of the Lost Ark*.
4. Humanize your anti-heroes and bad guys with a few sympathetic traits and/or give them a twisted moral code, such as they refuse to harm innocents.

THE OLD SWITCHEROO

Keep in mind the potential for great drama when one of the hero or villain's team is blackmailed or *willingly* switches sides. Are they double agents, in it for themselves, or had a change of heart?

MINOR CHARACTERS

"Minor characters can add spice to your novel, that extra spark that distinguishes the best fiction."

— JAMES SCOTT BELL, REVISION & SELF-EDITING

WE'VE TALKED ABOUT DEFINING the hero and villain's supporting cast. Now, let's take a look at minor characters and how they help flesh out your writer's world.

DEFINING MINOR CHARACTERS

Think about it: Would the scene in *The Empire Strikes Back* where Darth Vader hires Boba Fett have been as good without all the other bounty hunters in the background? Or the creepy bartender ghost Jack Nicholson talks to in *The Shining*? These guys may not get a lot of scenes, but they steal the ones they're in.

Why? Because minor characters ground the hero and villain in the setting. They show us how they interact with those who aren't on their level, but who still possess something they need.

"I always try to keep that in mind—that each minor character who comes on, even if it's only for one scene, has his own agenda, his own ideas, and he's not just there to serve the leads, so to speak."
—*George R. R. Martin*, "On the Craft of Writing"

MINOR CHARACTERS AREN'T ROCKET SCIENCE

They don't need as much development as your supporting cast, so it's often best to assign each minor character a "limp and an eye patch" and move on. By that, I mean a unique trait or two that makes them memorable: a foreign accent, a shifty-eyed look, or a peculiar outfit or hobby. Maybe the character always refers to himself in the third person, like George Remus, that annoying gangster from *Boardwalk Empire*. You get the idea.

HOW MINOR CHARACTERS TURN BORING SCENES GREAT

When your hero or villain enters a potentially boring scene with a minor character, be sure to consider that the minor character wants something too, and recognize the opportunity for conflict this represents.

For example, in Stanley Kubrick's *Eyes Wide Shut*, minor character Mr. Milich (Rade Serbedzija) refuses to let the hero, Dr. William Harford (Tom Cruise), into his costume shop after hours. While Harford grows increasingly desperate, Milich hems and haws, then finally agrees—but only *after* Harford bribes him. Milich then wastes the good doctor's time with weird stories and way too much personal information about his immoral daughter (Leelee Sobieski) and her Japanese "guests" before finally helping the doctor pick out the right costume.

This is a brilliant, hilarious scene and one people remember, even though it has *nothing* to do with the rest of the story. Milich inhabits his own little world. He has no connection to the secret sex club Harford is investigating. Milich exists simply to make a bit of extra trouble for the hero and to provide some much-needed comic relief, but of a kind that fits the disturbing tone of the film.

So the next day, when Dr. Harford returns his costume to the shop, the audience is delighted to see Milich and eager to find out what happened between him and his daughter after Harford left.

Be sure to have one or two scenes like this with minor characters in every story you write. They don't need to be long, they just need to be memorable.

If you are writing a series, find ways to bring the best of these minor characters back. For example, in my urban fantasy novel, *Titan*, I have the heroes summon the fussy ghost of a famous doctor to perform "psychic surgery" on a wounded character. The ghost advances the plot, but he also helps world-build the afterlife of my setting, as well as show off the power of the witch hero who summoned him. The ghost also provides some much-needed comic relief while still being a bit creepy. So naturally, when the heroes travel to the Underworld in the sequels, who they gonna call? No, not *Ghostbusters*! They're going to call the ghost doctor they met in the previous book.

Who knows? If your minor characters prove popular enough, they might merit their own spin-off series or standalone novels. After all, look what happened to Boba Fett: Fans loved him in *The Empire Strikes Back*, hated how he died in *Return of the Jedi*, and so LucasFilm brought him back to life in the *Star Wars* Expanded Universe, as well as for *Attack of the Clones*.

THAT'S IT for characters in general. We'll move on now to discuss the way gender impacts how characters think and feel. Buckle up, it's a bumpy ride...

— JDC

HOW TO WRITE REALISTIC MEN

INTRODUCTION

WHY DO SO MANY WRITERS FAIL to deliver credible, realistic male characters?

Male authors may introduce flat, one-dimensional action-hero types who always kick ass, get the girl, and win the day without ever revealing any true vulnerability. Sure, they may get captured, lose a few allies, and take hundreds of pages to take down the villain, but we don't ever learn anything about the character: his hopes and weaknesses, or what he really fears. These plot-driven books can be fun, but without character growth, the stories become forgettable cartoons.

Female authors may try to create idealized, fantasy versions of masculinity that they are more comfortable with. They don't understand how difficult it is to be a man—not because of our simplicity, but *because* of it. Idealized male characters will appear weak and way too open, both with themselves and with others—especially their love interests. They share their feelings, they aren't afraid to cry, and they don't get mad and storm out of the room or collapse into moody silence when shamed or confronted.

These are the unbelievable male characters that make male readers cringe. Even if the rest of the book is good, a single male character that rings false ruins it. No doubt the same case can be made for female readers who dislike the helpless caricatures many male authors sketch in for their hero's love interests.

In this next quick-start guide, I'm going to demystify male characters by revealing powerful secrets into the psychology of men. These secrets will take your writing to the next level with the complex, credible characters your fiction deserves!

— Jackson Dean Chase
Get a free book at
www.JacksonDeanChase.com

P.S.: This book deals in generalities and is not meant to be a blanket statement about gender. Exceptions to everything can and do exist. By first understanding the basics of how men think and act, it becomes easier to know how and why your male characters are the way they are. You'll also know what happens when your characters deviate from the basics—what they gain, what they lose, and why they think it's worth the trade-off.

WHAT MAKES A MAN A "MAN"

TO UNDERSTAND MEN, we first need to understand women. Women operate under many contradictory, complex rules. These rules create a vicious "shame web" that traps women no matter which way they turn, such as:

- "Work hard, but make it look effortless."
- "Dress sexy, but not slutty." (etc.)

Men, on the other hand, have only One Rule:

- "Don't be weak."

This is not the intricate ever-changing web of women, but a *rigid iron box*—a prison that tightly binds our responses. Every decision gets filtered through this One Rule. It doesn't matter if it's stupid, hurtful, or dangerous. And this happens even with the most enlightened, "in-touch with his feelings" kind of guy.

Why? Because he was raised by the One Rule. It's always there, lurking under the surface, no matter how much work he's done to break it. So while a sensitive, confident man may be able to ignore or reject the One Rule, he will always consider it, even if only on a subconscious level.

2

NATURE OR NURTURE

WHERE DID THE ONE RULE COME FROM? Is it nature or nurture? I believe it is both; the desire to compete, to dominate and control our surroundings—and defend our territory—is hardwired in. That desire is then consistently reinforced by other men; those we fear and those we love, both of whom encourage us to be bound by it or pay the cost.

In primitive days, no man wanted to go on a dangerous hunt or to war with a man he considered weak, because that weakness could get his fellow warriors injured or killed. A man had to be strong to contribute to his tribe, let alone attain a position of respect. The minute a leader showed weakness, he was either banished or killed. That's because men don't give up power easily. Few are willing to step down or aside, even to get out of their own way when it is in their best interest or that of their tribe.

What about demotion? Why does a man who loses his power have to be banished or killed? A man stripped of his power tends to harbor deep grudges. He will plot revenge. He will sow disharmony and do anything to make up for the humiliation of his failure.

Male pride demands revenge through the restoration of lost power. That means removing whoever got in his way and toppled him from his position. When revenge and/or restoration are not possible, a man's anger turns inward. He becomes bitter. Defeated. Morose. Petty. Stubborn. He will hate himself for his weakness and find small ways to act out against others, just to relieve the negative feelings that threaten to consume him.

WOMEN REINFORCE THE ONE RULE WITHOUT REALIZING IT

WOMEN SAY THEY WANT A KIND, caring, sensitive man—a man who can be vulnerable. And of course they do, but only to a certain extent. When a man dares to open himself up—to show how truly scared he is—the woman may reject him for not being a "real man."

Again, I believe this is because evolution has hardwired women to seek security for themselves and their offspring. A weak man is a threat to that security. He may not be able to physically protect them, nor be able to provide the resources needed for basic needs such as food and shelter.

A woman wants to take pride in her man, to prove to the rest of her tribe she is clever and attractive enough to catch and keep him. While the genders may express this pride in different ways, a man wants to take pride in his woman every bit as much. To pair with a good mate, a man must be strong and confident.

Sometimes, it seems men can't win. We have to be careful how we share and how much: just enough to be sensitive, but not enough to appear weak. This is a fine line to walk because as soon as a man feels rejected, he learns he can never truly reveal who he is, even to the woman he loves. This is a poison that can kill a relationship.

Men don't want to risk endangering their relationships, so many feel forced to put on an act, a constant strutting, preening show of strength to prevent other men from taking what they consider theirs: jobs, property, possessions, mates, etc.

The irony of course, is that a man who keeps his true self secret from others can ultimately end up losing everything: friends, family, even himself. His life is a charade and all his accomplishments ring hollow.

ANGER OR AVOIDANCE

BEING CONFINED BY THE ONE RULE leaves men two possible responses to shame: anger or emotional withdrawal. Pointing out actual or imagined weakness in a man triggers one of the two, which will eventually trigger the other if the man continues to feel disrespected. Remember, the greater the shame, the stronger the reaction.

Men don't like to feel forced to respond, and when pressured to do so, they may blow up or walk away rather than talk things out. *The One Rule demands it.*

At this stage, a man needs time to heal and get his "head together," sorting through the complex emotions of the situation. He may seek out others to commiserate with, typically other men he feels will offer loyalty and support without fear of judgment.

This healing process can take a few hours to a few days or more. It depends on the severity of the situation, how time-sensitive it is, and how quickly he can come up with solutions.

What are some things men do to blow off steam? Well, it depends on how angry or withdrawn they are. Common attempts at self-medication include the following actions, several of which may be tried or combined before finding the "right" ones:

- Alcohol
- Breaking things
- Cheating
- Criminal acts (speeding, vandalism, etc.)
- Driving, running, or walking aimlessly
- Drugs
- Fighting with people unrelated to the cause
- Sleep
- Sports (either watching or playing)
- Venting to people unrelated to friends
- Venting to family
- Video games
- Watching a movie or TV

Clearly, some actions are more high risk than others. A man prone to relying on one type of action will tend to return to it again and again, using it as a crutch to get him through.

This can be especially problematic if it is illegal or high-risk; if the man is caught or suffers in some way from taking the action, he will often blame the source of trouble that caused him to take the action: boss, coworker, family, friend, etc.

For example, a man in this position might say, "It's your fault I did it! You drove me to it with your bullshit. You just make me so crazy, I don't know what else to do."

Obviously, it's not the other person's fault, it's the man's for making a bad decision when he is not in the right frame of mind. But the One Rule doesn't let the man admit that to himself, not when there are convenient scapegoats nearby. Blaming others is a short-term fix to a long-term problem. It feels good in the moment because it doesn't strip away any more of the man's power at a time when he can least afford to lose it. This is toxic and can destroy a man if he's not careful.

The best thing to do is give a man time to think and heal on his own, then approach him hours later, or even better, wait for him to approach you. It will be hard for him; don't make it harder.

5

MEN FIX THINGS

WHEN PRESENTED WITH A PROBLEM, men prefer to solve the issue as quickly and easily as possible. We hate to hash over every tiny little detail, but desire to get to the heart of the matter and *fix it*. This minimizes the amount of time we may potentially appear weak. It may not always the best solution, but it is the one we are most comfortable with.

When a woman expresses confidence in our advice and ability to reach a solution, we feel powerful—respected and loved. We are in our element: a strong man fixing things. Any weakness we may have displayed (even if it was only in our own mind) is replaced by feelings of self-worth.

Unfortunately, men and women have different ways dealing with shame. This may cause gender miscommunication, such as in this familiar exchange:

Woman: "I just need you to listen to me!"

Man: "But how will that fix anything?"

But what these two are really saying is:

Woman: "I need to know you love and support me through anything."

Man: "I love you and hate seeing you hurt. It makes me feel weak to do nothing. I want to help by taking tangible, practical action. Let me either fix the problem for you, or help you fix it yourself, but let's do something about it right now."

Now that you understand the psychology of how men process shame and deal with problems, you have the framework not only to write convincing male characters, but to better understand the men in your life.

HOW MEN TALK AND ACT

WHEN NOT DEEP in male bonding, men tend to speak and gesture in bold, aggressive ways—these may stem from honest confidence to bluff and bravado.

Our drive to conquer and dominate is fueled by chemistry and culture so much that we find it difficult to stop—even when women react poorly to our words. That's because it's more important to appear strong to ourselves and those around us rather then modify our words and behavior.

Here are some typical male reactions to positive and negative events:

- "I crushed it!"
- "I killed it!"
- "I kicked their ass!"
- "BAM! In your face!"
- "Nailed it!"
- "Ha! You lose, sucker!"
- "You don't get it—they want to destroy me."
- "You want a war, you got a war!"
- "Are you trying to piss me off?"

- "What the hell were you thinking?"
- "They wouldn't dare!"
- "Nobody talks to me that way!"
- "That punk hasn't got the guts."
- "They all think I'm worthless, but I'll show them!"
- "Try that again and you'll be sorry."

You see the bold, violent way we talk? Men speak the language of war, a martial tongue fueled by the desire not just to compete, but control. Because deep down, we're scared if we can't control our environment, we're not strong enough to keep it. Everything is a battle at worst and a game at best. We feel if we could just say or do the right thing, everything else will fall into place and our victory will be assured.

Anything that challenges our position needs to be evaluated for how big a threat it is and how to deal with it quickly and decisively. We express our positions aggressively to not only show others our strength, but to reassure ourselves we can win.

Welcome to the deceptively simple yet unbelievably complicated world of men.

HOW TO WRITE MALE BONDING SCENES

MEN RARELY SIT DOWN with the goal of talking about our emotions. Instead, opening up occurs as a by-product of engaging in another activity such as sports, drinking, etc. The activity makes it safer for us to bring up our problems, as attention can quickly return to the activity if our attempt meets with rejection.

When we feel comfortable, we let our guard down—but only with people we trust. The One Rule is always lurking as we consider how to express our feelings in a way that does not violate the rule. Sometimes words are difficult, and all we can manage are sighs, grunts, or curses. Body language may be used to emphasize mood, such as rubbing our head or chin, putting our face in our hands, or making frustrated gestures. Slumped shoulders are also common.

This is the cue for the listener to begin some vague and gentle questioning to determine what the problem is. The troubled man will use carefully chosen words, often in coded language interspersed with more non-verbal communication (such as long drinks of beer) to allow space to test the listener's response.

Should he not be rejected or ridiculed (at least not too badly), the troubled man may continue to open up. This is when the touching, tender, revealing part of the bonding scene happens, but he will still be cautious, talking *around* his "weakness" until he can come to the heart of the matter. His emotions will cycle between confusion, frustration, fear, and anger.

Now it is the listener's turn to offer advice and encouragement in an attempt at problem-solving. He may offer anecdotes from his own life in an attempt to put the troubled man at ease and provide reassurance he's not the only one to have this problem.

Note that men will use terms such as "bro," "man," or "dude" to express affection in a way that reinforces strength and camaraderie while downplaying weakness. A man rarely says, "I love you," to other men not related to him because that could be perceived as weakness even though it is actually strength.

Most expressions of love among men must pass through the One Rule's filter and come out translated as quick, rough hugs, arm punches, or slaps on the back, often accompanied by "I love you, man," "You're the best, dude," "You got this!" or "You deserve it, bro."

Rarely will a man cry, and when he does, it will usually be when he is sure he is alone. However, if his need is too great, he may cry in front of a best friend, family member, or a trusted father-figure. As a guideline, the only other time male tears are publicly acceptable is for a sports victory, especially a championship.

When a man begins to tear up, he may try to divert attention through an action such as grabbing another beer, looking away, lying or joking that he has "some dust in his eye," going to another room, or leaving the location and not returning until he has his emotions under control.

When a man feels he's reached his emotional limit or the problem has been resolved, he will offer brief, guarded appreciation to the other man for listening. The exchange will end with reassuring "manly" sayings and/or gestures as indicated above. In more formal situations (such as with a mentor about a career problem), a heartfelt handshake may suffice.

This is the signal for both men to ease back into the boundaries of the One Rule by making fun of themselves and/or the problem.

Shared humor reinforces that the men are strong enough to laugh off this danger and have become stronger by talking it out.

Contrast this with the way women relate with each other. With them, weakness is not a concern and affection is easily given, but solutions may take longer to appear, perhaps only after multiple discussions.

HOW TO WRITE REALISTIC WOMEN

INTRODUCTION

IN THIS THIRD AND FINAL QUICK START GUIDE, I'm going to teach you the top secrets of how to create fully realized, three-dimensional female heroes and villains. I'm going to give you all the same resources, the same research, but I'm going to deliver it in bite-size chunks, with practical examples of the very real and very different challenges women face that men don't. If you're a man (and I assume you are), some of these challenges you may be aware of, others you may not.

Let me shoot the elephant in the room: This is not a boring, politically correct manifesto on feminism or social justice or anything like that. There are plenty of in-depth books on gender equality and women's issues by far more qualified writers. What this book does is provide a unique toolkit for male authors to learn how to write realistic women in the easiest and shortest way possible.

Why should you do this? Beyond the obvious goal of being a better, more well-rounded writer and providing strong role models, there is another incentive—a financial one. Women read more books than men and they also write more reviews. Not just by a little bit, but by a lot! And women naturally want to see themselves reflected in your words. That can't happen if you don't know the secrets contained in this book. These secrets are how you win over female readers, sell more copies, and get better reviews. So don't wimp out.

Are you ready? It's time to man up and write realistic women!

— Jackson Dean Chase
Get a free book at
www.JacksonDeanChase.com

P.S.: Just another reminder this book deals in generalities and is not meant to be a blanket statement about gender. Exceptions to everything can and do exist. By first understanding the basics of how women think and act, it becomes easier to know how and why your female characters are the way they are.

You'll also know what happens when your characters deviate from the basics—what they gain, what they lose, and why they think it's worth the trade-off.

GENDER DIFFERENCES IN STORYTELLING

WHEN I WAS RESEARCHING my first novel, I came across Christopher Vogler's *The Writer's Journey: Mythic Structure for Writers*, a book that put the storytelling theory of Professor Joseph Campbell into an easily accessible, digestible formula for writers. It's a great book, but focused solely on the male perspective—which was a problem, since I was writing a novel with a female main character. Then I stumbled across Kim Hudson's *The Virgin's Promise: Writing Stories of Feminine Creative, Spiritual, and Sexual Awakening*. This presented a feminine take on Campbell's theory—again, for writers—and it really opened my eyes to gender differences in storytelling. While men's stories are all about defeating external evil and saving *others*, women's stories are much more about defeating internal evil and saving *themselves*.

In other words, most masculine stories adhere to mythic structure, while most feminine stories adhere to fairy tale structure. That's not to say men can't go on "feminine" journeys (such as Lester Burnham does in *American Beauty*) or women can't go on "masculine" ones (such as Dorothy *The Wizard of Oz*). Part of the fun of being a writer is deciding which kind of journey you want your main character to go on.

MASCULINE AND FEMININE HEROIC JOURNEYS

To differentiate between the two types, *The Virgin's Promise* refers to a female main character going on a feminine journey as a "virgin" (the term in this context isn't sexually-related, but refers to the heroine's unawakened, inexperienced state). The author explains the story difference as:

> The quest of the Virgin is to become all she is capable of being and in so doing create joy and happiness. The quest of the Hero is to assert his will against evil and in so doing overcome fear.
> —Kim Hudson, *The Virgin's Promise*

Ms. Hudson goes on to illustrate there are other differences too, most strikingly in the stakes involved:

> The tensions are also different in the Virgin and Hero stories. The cost of the Virgin going on her pathway is the potential loss of love, joy, and passion. Without these things that accompany the fulfillment of her dream, the Virgin suffers loss of self, which manifests as depression, insanity or suicide. The cost to the Hero going on his journey is potentially death. This loss of life at the hands of others will involve physical pain and leave his village vulnerable to evil.

So the Virgin is not likely to die except by her own hand, and neither is her village necessarily doomed (indeed, they may not even understand there is a problem at all). The Hero, on the other hand, has an *extremely* high chance of being killed by his enemies, and everyone in his village understands they will suffer too if he fails. As Kim Hudson explains it:

> Both stories follow an emotional pattern in which the protagonist is at first tenuous, then takes a chance and almost loses, but learns from this experience and finally follows the pathway to success. In short,

they both go through emotional reversals that make for great storytelling."

Until I read *The Writer's Journey* and *The Virgin's Promise*, I was blind to the fundamental gender differences in storytelling. But my journey didn't end there...

2

HOW I LEARNED TO WRITE FEMALE CHARACTERS

WHEN I SET out to write my first novel, I did the math and figured I'd make the main character female. Women buy more books, therefore they must want to read about women. But why would they want to read about ones written by a man? And me specifically?

The problem was, even though I'd been around women my whole life—*had dated them, lived with them, been friends*—I didn't know much about them. Oh sure, I knew they were different than guys, but I had no idea *why*.

If I was going to write an authentic female, it was time to find out!

WHERE TO BEGIN?

I'd always loved *Mean Girls* (underdog stories are my favorite), so I started my research by reading *Queen Bees and Wannabes* by Rosalind Wiseman, the non-fiction book the movie was (loosely) based on. That was revealing, but only whet my appetite for more. A female friend recommended *Reviving Ophelia* by Mary Pipher, and that was helpful too. Brené Brown's *Daring Greatly* further added to my understanding of the complicated, spiraling "shame web" that surrounds women (men, on the other hand, get a prison-type box to hide our shame in).

To quickly summarize, Brown says men live by one rule: "Don't be weak," while women live by an endless supply of contradictory rules: "Dress sexy, but don't look like a slut," etc. And here I thought the one rule men live by was hard—at least it doesn't contradict itself! Since I was writing a dark, edgy book, I also read memoirs like Kerry Cohen's *Loose Girl: A Memoir of Promiscuity* and chick-lit like Martha O'Connor's *The Bitch Posse*. I watched all the hip teen girl shows like *Pretty Little Liars, The Lying Game, Twisted*, etc. Through combining everything I'd learned from all these sources, I quickly and easily learned how female characters acted and reacted to various situations, how they related to others, even to themselves.

Another key book for me was *45 Master Characters* by Victoria Lynn Schmidt, which compared and contrasted the feminine heroic journey vs. the masculine one: the differences in power and support, and how the genders start off in essentially different worlds: Both men and women need to dissolve their ego to awaken. Women *come into* their power to realize their authentic goals and connectedness, whereas men *let go* of their power to realize their authentic goals and connectedness.

> The awakening is like a form of surrender the character goes through,
> a rebirth into the unknown.
> —Victoria Lynn Schmidt, *45 Master Characters*

This was amazing, fascinating stuff! I was beginning to feel confident I could create complex, believable female characters of any age.

Of course, no book on how to write female characters would be complete without mentioning the Bechdel Test, which is a way to gauge a work's gender bias by asking the following questions:

1. Does the story have at least two women in it,
2. who talk to each other,
3. about something *besides* a man.

A fourth question is often added that asks if these characters are named or not, indicating whether they have any level of importance or not.

Doing this research into writing realistic women not only made me a better writer, it made me a better man, and a better friend to the women in my life.

THE EASY TWO-STEP FORMULA TO WRITING REALISTIC WOMEN

IN *A GAME of Thrones* and its sequels, best selling author George R. R. Martin created some of the most realistic, beloved female characters in fiction. With the notable and annoying exception of Sansa Stark, Martin creates strong female heroes that are a pleasure to read. He does that by making them interesting people who struggle with incredibly complex, dangerous problems—problems that appeal to all readers first and to "women's issues" second.

In fact, most of Martin's "women's issues" aren't boring domestic obligations, pregnancy, or anything like that, but instead they are additional complications to how the character's problems must be solved because they are women operating in a ruthless medieval patriarchy. Because they are women, how they wield power is different than how a man would wield it. The end result may be the same, but how it happens behind the scenes tends to require extra scheming and consensus-building.

If the female character fails to take into account all the fragile male egos involved—and how to juggle them against her own needs—then she is likely to face rebellion, betrayal, or worse far faster than if she were a man.

Because Martin writes his other female characters so well, his

Sansa Stark chapters stick out as exceptionally boring. Sansa starts weak and stays weak. Her chapters are so dull and whiney and involved solely with "women problems," so much that they are unrelatable to male readers. When my friends and I compared notes, we discovered we all skimmed or skipped her chapters, and doing that made no impact on our understanding the story— that means her chapters were essentially worthless. We never dared do that with any of the other female characters—in fact, we looked forward to them.

The writers of the HBO adaptation wisely altered Sansa's character to learn from her unique situation; over the course of the series, she slowly transforms from annoying teenager to calculating political player. If Martin had done that in his books, I guarantee my friends and I wouldn't have skipped Sansa's chapters.

But George R. R. Martin isn't alone in making this mistake. Many male writers think a female character must be obsessed with "women's issues." It's no wonder I cringe whenever my favorite movies or TV shows switch from showing the men involved in danger and fun to show the wives or girlfriends being shrill and boring.

That's because women's problems often revolve around boring domestic issues which cause the characters to come off as burdensome nags that do nothing to advance the plot. Their sole function in the story seems to be to "ground" the male characters in some sense of normalcy to serve as a contrast to their exciting away from home adventures. Either that, or to do something incredibly stupid that gets the men in trouble because the female characters don't understand the stakes or subscribe to some blind, naïve world view.

Think Carmela Soprano, Charmaine Bucco, and the other wives from *The Sopranos* (TV, 1999-2007). Compared to the colorful, exciting male Mafia characters, these women are neither likable nor interesting (at least to men), but they sure take up a lot of screen time. The girlfriends and mistresses get to be a little more fun, but not much. That's because they're bit players designed to titillate viewers with sex while complicating the male characters' already complicated lives.

How many wives and girlfriends—or women in general—from

your favorite movies, TV, books, or comics can you think of who are interesting, dynamic plot movers and shakers? Probably not many, at least not without having to think hard. The only female characters I can remember liking on *The Sopranos* were Tony's suicidal mistress, Gloria, Christopher's nightclub-owning girlfriend, Adriana, and of course, Tony's psychiatrist, Dr. Melfi.

Why? Because these women are the rewards men get, while the wives are the "punishment." But if you take away the men, none of these women would have any impact on the series. They don't have their own stories, not really.

The obvious solution would be to find a way to bring in one or more female criminals, especially one who heads up a rival or allied operation, and one who is just as dastardly as any of Tony's crew. This happens in season two of *The Sopranos*, when Tony goes to Italy and meets a Mafia family run by a woman, and it's beyond wonderful. Unfortunately, her storyline is not continued, and no other female master criminals emerge throughout the rest of the series to take her place.

Of course, no discussion of *The Sopranos* would be complete without mentioning Tony's mom, Livia. This is a strong female character. Her storyline impacts not only the plot, but Tony's entire backstory. She's the reason he has to see Dr. Melfi. Without Livia, there is no special reason why Tony is different from any other mob boss. He'd still be entertaining, but he wouldn't be as nearly as deep and rich a character.

Here's the problem: Livia is a villain. She presents a deliciously real, credible threat to Tony—not just physically (through plotting to have him killed), but mentally and emotionally (through psychologically torturing him his entire life). Livia is definitely a character you'll never forget, and her influence is felt long after she's dead. But villains don't have to be likable, they just have to make viewers love to hate them.

We'll touch on how female villains operate later, but the biggest problem most writers face is getting readers to feel sympathy not just for female heroes, but female *anti-heroes*. Anytime you have women behave outside gender expectations, it's easy to run into trouble. Nowhere is this more prevalent than when writing anti-heroes. A man behaving badly is applauded while a woman behaving the same is not.

House of Cards (TV, 2013-present) attempts to make the male protagonist's wife, Claire, a compelling character and antihero like her husband, but with mixed results. She's mildly interesting as his scheming confidante and ally, but completely cold and unlikable—never more than when her subplot veers into typical boring women's issues, such as when she cheats on her husband, separates from him, and then causes all kinds of annoying, unnecessary political problems. There might have been a way to make that interesting, but the show fails to do that. We'll go into more detail about female antiheroes later, including what makes them tick and how to make them likable.

Let's get back to talking about heroes. For one of my favorite examples, let's examine *The Rockford Files* (TV, 1974-1980). Hard luck private eye, Jim Rockford (James Garner), is brought a case by well-meaning but shifty lawyer, Beth Davenport (Gretchen Corbett). Beth is an early example of the strong female hero. She's tough-minded and tenacious, putting people before profits which comes into conflict with Jim's mercenary nature. Jim can smell her coming a mile away and groans inwardly every time because he knows what it means... trouble. As a result of her legal crusades, Beth is always getting in over her head and dragging poor Jim along for the ride.

Why do we love her? Beth has an interesting career, charming character flaws, and more importantly, without her bringing Jim all these crazy, horrible cases, there'd be no story. On top of that, she matches Jim word for word in witty banter and constantly outsmarts him by skipping out on what she promised to pay (for noble reasons, though I'm sure Jim would beg to differ). Hell, Beth could have her own series without Jim and I'd watch it. Later on, when the two of them get romantically involved, it's magic. Why? Because the audience has come to love and respect Beth as an interesting person first and as a woman second.

~

So what does all this teach us? The trick to writing women that people care about is to follow a simple two-step formula.

STEP 1:
First, make sure your female characters are:
a) interesting people
b) struggling with interesting problems
c) in interesting ways, and

STEP 2:
Make them female.

How do you do that? By making sure your female characters have their own dreams, goals, and desires separate from their romantic relationships with men, and that they have interesting strengths and flaws and quirks and every reason to be in your story.

They cannot exist solely as sidekicks, love interests, or background players. If you want them to be awesome, their actions *must* advance the plot.

Here's another way of looking at it: If you can replace your female character with a lamp for all the good she does, then guess what? *You're not writing realistic women.*

HIDDEN PITFALLS OF THE STRONG FEMALE HERO

MANY MALE WRITERS fall into the trap of writing their female heroes like "men with boobs." Don't be one of them. Don't put a strong woman in your story to help it sell, to be "PC," or because you think it's sexy. Just like with any story, the only reason to put a strong female in is if it needs one. She must contribute in meaningful ways that actively move the plot forward. As I've said before, she does this by being an interesting character first and a woman second.

Whatever you do, do not interpret the word "strong" literally. Your female hero doesn't need to be physically equal to men, she just needs to be as smart and as determined, and to have agency of her own.

Even if she's an action hero, she's not necessarily going to be as strong as her toughest male adversaries, though as female body builders have proven, she can certainly come close. It's likely she will compensate with increased cunning and speed, as well as specialized training. She will also be likely to take advantage of the fact that males frequently underestimate female opponents in combat. They hesitate, either from an ingrained societal command not to hurt "the weaker sex" or, if they're bastards, from taking a moment to gloat over the idea of an easy victory. Then, when they realize the fight will be harder than they thought, they get mad. Anger leads to mistakes, which leads to failure. Their shame is not just losing, but losing to a woman.

The strong female's role cannot be to give herself up, to sit around whining and waiting to be rescued, or to lead the male hero to a "higher plane," as in so many love stories and fairy tales like *Cinderella, Rapunzel,* or *Sleeping Beauty.*

She is not the object of the quest, but the one who takes the quest.

Though the quest can (and should) have many components, it must ultimately be about the female's self-realization and self-empowerment. She must shatter whatever male-dominated bonds she had at the beginning and, win or lose, be free to make her own choices at the end.

In a tragedy, she will give up her freedom (and perhaps her life) to help free others even if only by example (such as Joan of Arc).

In a happy ending, she keeps her hard-won freedom and uses it to benefit herself and others. There must be a price to pay and there will be scars (emotional or otherwise), but the woman becomes transformed by her quest. She comes into herself and her power, forcing the people around her to value and respect her on her terms, not theirs.

Beyond the strong female's internal struggle, the way she gears up for her external struggle and assembles her team is different than men. When practical, there will be more planning, talking, listening, and consensus-building, as that's how women tend to get things done. They rarely can bully their way into leadership positions, so they have to be smart about it and consider the feelings of others—or at least pretend to.

The strong female will arm herself sensibly, and select weapons suited to her ability and skill set. And, perhaps most importantly, she will dress sensibly... no chainmail bikinis, no skimpy spandex costumes that show off her body. But why not? Isn't that how women are portrayed when they go into battle? Sure, but have you ever asked yourself *why* they're depicted that way?

Because of the male gaze.

What's that? If you're a woman, you know exactly what it is and how it effects you every day of your life. But if you're a man, you're probably oblivious, so let's break it down.

THE MALE GAZE

THE MALE GAZE is the way men in a patriarchal society see and evaluate women from the first moment they meet, distorting their perceived value by how sexually attractive they appear. The less attractive, the less value, up to the point where the woman ceases to be seen as her gender at all, but some sort of invisible "it." And an "it" is tolerated at best, then mocked for her lack of gender and attractiveness as soon as her back is turned.

The male gaze sees women first and foremost as objects of pleasure, and secondarily as passive, submissive, and largely irrelevant "support units" compared to their active, domineering male counterparts. When women attempt to break free from these male misconceptions, they are met with resentment ("what a bitch!"), condescension (aka mansplaining), or increased sexual attention.

Whether that male attention is an honest expression of heightened interest and attraction or used as a weapon to put the woman in "her place," the problem is that men are viewing her through the male gaze and not evaluating her ideas or other contributions objectively.

The male gaze pollutes pop culture and all aspects of the media by trivializing women, infantilizing them, and holding them up to impossible ideals—not just of beauty, but of who women can be at home, in the workplace, in relationships—basically in all aspects of their lives.

There is a true power disparity here, and is it any wonder that this patriarchal enforcement of gender stereotypes breeds so much unhappiness and confusion? Is it really so mysterious that women still suffer the burden of navigating our male-dominated society? Of being paid less, charged more, then hitting the glass ceiling and told sorry, that's as far as you get?

Imagine how you would feel if a bunch of oppressive, aggressive men told you what you could do with your body and what your rights were? These men use everything they have to keep you down, from religion to politics to business to culture, all in the name of "protecting" you when they are really only protecting themselves. They use media to control you, to brainwash you into conforming to what they think you should look like and how you must behave.

Imagine how crazy-making it would be to receive a constant stream of conflicting advice: "look sexy, but not too sexy," or "work hard, but make it look effortless." And not just to hear this from men, but other women as well!

That's because some women, not seeing any other choice, "go along to get along." They resent it when they see other women break that mold and will attempt to stop them. It's the old analogy of "crabs in a barrel"—when the captured crabs spot one of their own climbing out of the barrel, they pull her back down to suffer alongside them.

As if that wasn't bad enough, now consider how women's personal safety and right to go about their day unmolested is constantly challenged by men, from catcalls of "Hey, baby!" to serious attempts to seduce you wherever you go. A woman sitting alone in a bar is seen as in need of a man, while a man in a bar simply needs a drink.

And then there's the danger of being assaulted or raped. That is why women think twice about walking down dark alleys or through deserted parking lots. It's also one of the reasons they travel in groups —not just for the social aspects, but so they can look out for each other.

When women do get into relationships with men, they may run

into him resenting her if she makes more money or tries to take too much control. Then there's the risk of the man only wanting her for sex, and the risk of her getting pregnant. Even if things go well, over time, as the woman ages and her attention shifts from him to their children or other responsibilities, the man's eyes might wander to a younger, sexier woman. Women are never safe from the male gaze—whether it is directed at them or others.

When many male writers try to create active, strong female heroes, their vision is still clouded by the male gaze. They simply superimpose "strong" male personality traits over sexually idealized female bodies. The results are cartoon characters whose "strength" is judged by how many men they can seduce, manipulate, or physically defeat in traditionally masculine ways.

So how do male writers create strong female characters? The obvious way is to make her not so much about her appearance, but who she is on the inside. This is the plucky plain Jane who succeeds in a male-dominated world despite her "failure" to arouse the male gaze, at least in a conventional sense.

Think Peggy Olson (Elisabeth Moss) from *Mad Men* (TV, 2007-2015). Over the course of the series, Peggy rises up from lowly secretary to advertising executive. And she has to do it the hard way, by proving the strength of her ideas all while constantly being put down, resented, or ignored by her male counterparts. Because the male gaze devalues Peggy, every day for her is a struggle. And when she screws up (even if it isn't really her fault), she can't fall back on her sexuality to save her. She's likely to be demoted, fired, or humiliated with impunity by the men around and above her.

Because of her gender, Peggy has to work twice as hard to get the same rewards and even then, usually has to settle for less pay, less prestige. She is seen as an anomaly because of her sex and her ambition to compete in a traditionally male job. She may even be pitied by other women because she is busy working instead of finding a husband and raising children.

Do you ever wonder why so female characters in books written by women are described as plain or otherwise atypically appealing to men? Because when a male character falls for her, and/or when he learns to respect and value her, it's not for what she looks like: *It's for who she is.*

Should all your female characters be plain or homely? Of course not! A less obvious and more challenging way to write a strong female is to make it *more* about her appearance, not less. But the trick here is the story is about her having to deal with the constant annoyance of the male gaze and how what she is seen as and lusted after by them conflicts with who she is on the inside.

Mad Men provides another perfect example in Joan Harris (Christina Hendricks), who rises up from being head of the secretarial pool and the mistress of one the ad agency's founders to being a partner in the agency. She has plenty of brains, talent, and ambition under all that sexuality, and uses everything she has to get what she wants. But given the choice, Joan prefers to use her brains more than her body. Even though she appreciates her sexuality's usefulness, she hates herself for having to rely on it to get ahead. But because men enjoy looking at her, Joan would have to do something pretty stupid to ever be demoted, fired, or otherwise humiliated.

Because the male gaze values her, Joan's life is easier than Peggy's in some ways and harder in others. She has to fight to be heard because "any woman that pretty can't be smart," and then when she is finally heard, she has to struggle with the result of that success, which is the man she is influencing wanting to sleep with her—even feeling like "she owes it to him" for helping her! And if Joan does not return that affection, the man may lash out and renege on his promises.

Using seduction and manipulation becomes part of Joan's strategy —not because she'd be a fool not to use it—but because men simply give her no choice. She has something they want, and as long as they stay interested and she can keep that sexual tension going, those men are far more likely to do what she says. The risk with this strategy is when one or more of the men insist on her giving them what they want. Even if she rejects him and gets what she wants, others will still accuse her of sleeping her way to the top because "that's the only way a woman who looks like her can get what she wants."

Because of her beauty, Joan's short-term challenges are easier to overcome than Peggy's, but Peggy has the long-term career advantage: Because the men she is dealing with most likely do not want to sleep with her, they have to at least grudgingly come to value and respect her as a person. Maybe not as much as a man, but close enough where she can get more or less get what she wants eventually, though she will always have to keep fighting... if not the old guard, then all the men coming up under her who have not learned to respect her yet.

As Joan ages and her beauty fades, her ability to influence men diminishes because the male gaze values youth as well as as beauty. Because she relied on her sexuality to get ahead, her ability to get what she wants through who she is instead of what she is will not be as advanced as Peggy's. This ticking clock says women get less sexy as they age and its the primary reason Joan pushes so hard to get what she wants as fast as possible. Since the clock has far less effect on Peggy, she can afford to take the long view more than Joan.

Makes sense? Great! But maybe you don't write workplace dramas like *Mad Men*. Maybe you write science fiction or fantasy. Everything I teach in this book applies as long as your world roughly conforms to our own past or present. Things only change if your society moves from a patriarchy to a gynarchy or a gender-neutral society based on individual merit.

"THERE CAN BE ONLY ONE!"

FORGET WHAT *HIGHLANDER* TAUGHT YOU. One of the biggest problems male writers run into is only including a single strong female character. Why is that a problem? Because then she becomes a token, an anomaly. You can point to her and say, "See? I'm a feminist! I put a strong female hero in my story." Um, no. You need to put more than one strong female character in your story to pass the Bechdel Test.

The second female doesn't have to be the same kind of hero as the first, and it's often better if she isn't. For example (again), Peggy Olson and Joan Harris in *Mad Men*.

In a fantasy, you could make one woman a barbarian warrior, the other a thief and wizard, like a female version of Fritz Lieber's legendary Fafhrd and the Gray Mouser.

In a science fiction story, make one woman a tough space marine and the other a cunning warrant officer. Think Jenette Vasquez and Ellen Ripley in *Aliens* (1986)—they're both strong, but they're very different characters.

But if you want them to be the same, you can. Think Robert E. Howard's Conan the Barbarian and Red Sonja or Xena and Gabrielle from *Xena: Warrior Princess* (TV, 1995-2001). They're all warriors, but they were raised differently, trained differently, and have different fighting styles. Regardless of what makes them different, what keeps them together?

Bonus points if you include three or more strong female characters in your story. Three? Maybe that seems like a lot, but it really isn't. Again, you should find a way to differentiate your characters both personally and professionally.

Think Captain Kirk, Mr. Spock, and Dr. McCoy from *Star Trek* (TV, 1966-69). Kirk's bold, Spock's logical, and McCoy's a skeptic. They complement each other and it is the combination of their skills and personalities that allows them to survive. Plus, the endless bickering, jokes, insults, and rivalries are hilarious.

Now that you've got the concept, there's no reason you can't do that with female characters. Think *Buffy the Vampire Slayer* (TV, 1997-2003), *Charmed* (TV, 1998-2006), *The Vampire Diaries* (TV, 2009-2017), or *Pretty Little Liars* (TV, 2010-present). Each of these shows found a successful way to incorporate multiple strong female heroes.

THE PROBLEM OF THE MARY SUE
AND MANIC PIXIE DREAM GIRL

IT WOULD BE remiss of me not to mention—and to caution you against using—two of the most common (and hated) tropes writers resort to when creating female characters:

1. the "Mary Sue" and
2. the "Manic Pixie Dream Girl"

Many women hate these tropes because they are gimmicks, not reality. But not all women hate them, of course, and not all men. Of the two, women prefer the Mary Sue, while men prefer the Manic Pixie Dream Girl. I believe that is because each offers a specific type of wish fulfillment:

- What woman does not want to be perfect and find her perfect love?
- What man does not want to fall in love with a fun, adventurous woman that helps him become a better man?

The Mary Sue has no meaningful flaws. She may start in a lowly position, but she is already "perfect" as a woman and a hero. The reason Mary Sues don't work is they have no depth.

While there is a certain amount of controversy and debate around who is (or isn't) a Mary Sue, some of the best known examples being discussed on the internet are:

- Cinderella from *Cinderella* (1950)
- Princess Aurora from *Sleeping Beauty* (1959)
- Lara Croft in *Tomb Raider* (2001)
- Bella Swan in *Twilight* (2009)
- Elena Gilbert from *The Vampire Diaries* (TV, 2009-2017)
- Katniss Everdeen from *The Hunger Games* (2012)
- Beatrice "Tris" Prior from *Divergent* (2014)
- Imperator Furiosa from *Mad Max: Fury Road* (2015)
- Rey from *Star Wars: The Force Awakens* (2015)

As you can see from this list, Mary Sues are pure of heart and good at everything they do. They are the "chosen ones," destined by birth or circumstance for some epic love or grand adventure that will change the world, but why? It's certainly not their personality! Mary Sues may be pretty, they may be talented, but there's no special reason to like or follow them, and certainly not to love them.

Isn't charisma important? Charm? Personal magnetism? Mary Sues exhibit few to none of these qualities. They are stand-ins for the author and reader, offering wish-fulfillment, nothing more.

Want to find out if your character is a Mary Sue? Take the Bechdel Test free online (Google is your friend).

THE MANIC PIXIE Dream Girl is a free spirit, a love interest who comes into the male hero's life and turns it upside down with her girlish charm and ridiculous quirkiness. By forcing him out of the rut his life is in, she leads him to a higher plane but often disappears or dies at the end. And no one cares. The Manic Pixie Dream Girl doesn't work because she is only in the story to help the male character change. She's a plot device, not a real character.

Some of the wackiest and best known examples of the Manic Pixie Dream Girl are:

- Susan Vance from *Bringing Up Baby* (1938)
- Sugar "Kane" Kowalczyk from *Some Like It Hot* (1959)
- Holly Golightly from *Breakfast at Tiffany's* (1961)
- Annie Hall from *Annie Hall* (1977)
- Vivianne from *Pretty Woman* (1990)
- Belle from *Beauty and the Beast* (1991)
- Mary from *There's Something About Mary* (1998)
- Penny Lane from *Almost Famous* (2000)
- Polly Prince from *Along Came Polly* (2004)

While the characters in these examples may be fun and exciting in a temporary sense, they are ethereal bits of nothing, childish fluff that's impossible to cling to.

Manic Pixie Dream Girls don't live in the real world, but rather one of their own invention that has a completely different set of rules. Maybe that's why they won't (or can't) stick around, and we're better off when they're gone.

Honestly, these characters remind me more of *The Cat in the Hat* by Dr. Seuss than anything else, and like the Cat, they can be just as troublesome, even dangerous when you apply their wacky schemes to reality.

Looking for ways to know if your character is a Manic Pixie Dream Girl?

ANOTHER WAY TO tell if you've written a Mary Sue or Manic Pixie Dream Girl is to see if they have a character arc. If your character doe not grow and change in a dramatic and meaningful way, she may be a Mary Sue or Manic Pixie Dream Girl. Then again, she may simply be a catalyst hero, one who comes into the story already fully formed. A catalyst's mission is to force the other characters to arc. Catalysts are more common to series than standalones.

Note that by "fully formed" I don't mean flawless. For example, James Bond has several deep character flaws he seldom bothers to examine, much less rein in. He glories in them instead (misogyny, narcissism, and racism). Dirty Harry is another series character written in a similar vein. It is these flaws that make them interesting and prevent them from being the male equivalent of Mary Sues.

So why aren't more female series characters expressing similar flaws? Why are they stuck being perfect and perfectly boring? Is it because people are more willing to accept—even embrace—negative qualities in a man, but not in a woman? Is there a double standard, and if so, can it be broken?

FEMALE ANTI-HEROES: A SLOW
SLIDE INTO HELL

A RECENT THEORY suggests there may be key differences in the way men and women hate (and forgive). If true, these play a critical difference in how your characters react. According to the theory:

- Men tend to hate groups for life, but find it easier to forgive individuals.
- Women tend to hate individuals for life, but find it easier to forgive groups.

The reason for this may be hardwiring from our primitive past, a past where men relied more on certain key individuals for survival where women relied on groups. Because men have traditionally had more agency and freedom to act, they feel empowered to continue taking revenge far beyond the individual level. Whereas women have not had the same agency, and therefore tend to limit themselves to "safe," small-scale revenge. You can see this difference played out in to this day in modern revenge stories.

In the *Death Wish* series (1974-1994), architect Paul Kersey (Charles Bronson) takes a stand against criminals. Once he serves up vigilante justice to the scum who raped and murdered his wife and daughter, he doesn't stop there. He keeps hunting criminals completely unrelated to his personal revenge. He can't stop because he has nothing left to live for; killing becomes his identity.

In the *Dirty Harry* series (1971-1988), cop Harry Callahan (Clint Eastwood) has a similar problem with crime; crime briefly personified by the villain(s) of each film, but his war is never over. There's always more crime to fight. And both Kersey and Callahan have another group to hate: the justice system, for its failure to help the innocent and for letting violent criminals go on technicalities.

Compare that to Beatrix Kiddo (Uma Thurman) in *Kill Bill* (2003), who is only interested in avenging herself on the specific individuals who wronged her. She kills others, sure, but just to get to the names on her list. Or Jennifer (Camille Keaton) in *I Spit On Your Grave* (1978), who is content to stop being a vigilante after she avenges herself on her rapists.

Exceptions of women hating groups certainly exist, like Thana (Zoe Tamerlis) in *Ms. .45* (1981), who becomes a deranged vigilante killer, or Carrie White (Sissy Spacek) in *Carrie* (1976), who seeks a wider revenge beyond just her immediate bullies, murdering the entire school who humiliated her.

The differences in how the genders hate and forgive may also play a role in how female anti-heroes are received. People expect to be entertained by men acting out of control, but when they see a woman do it? Not so much. That's where gender bias comes in.

Audiences love to watch male anti-heroes like Tony Soprano (*The Sopranos*), Don Draper (*Mad Men*), and Walter White (*Breaking Bad*, (TV, 2008-2013) do all kinds of shitty things. They expect it, they want it, they demand it! And it does little to change the character's likability. But when a female character does something similar, she's often hated. Whatever respect or affection audiences may have had for her goes right out the window. (Case in point: Skyler White on *Breaking Bad*.)

Because women are supposed to be likable, she's instantly and forever hated. Especially by men. They see her as a traitor, a nag, a bitch, a dummy, a whore, even a lunatic! But most importantly, they see her as a *killjoy*. Her only purpose in the story is rewired in the male mind as to stop men from having fun. And while female audiences will likely take the opposite view, that doesn't mean they always will if the character's actions violate too many of the "rules" of being a woman. In short, it's complicated.

I love to write dark, complex female anti-heroes with villainous tendencies. The way I succeed is by not starting off in that dark place. I slowly introduce her to the reader in likable ways. Likable, but flawed. As she continues to pursue her goals, she feels forced to take increasingly drastic actions. The more drastic the action, the more delusional my anti-hero becomes trying to justify what she's doing is the right thing, the only thing. Eventually, she snaps, and that's when the real fun begins...

This strategy only works because I took the time to set it up. It's a slow slide into hell, never a sudden about-face. That's how you win audiences over to your female anti-hero: warming them up.

For strong female anti-heroes audiences of both genders love, I recommend watching Veronica Sawyer from *Heathers* (1988), Gemma Teller-Morrow from *Sons of Anarchy* (TV, 2008-2014), and Norma Bates from *Bates Motel* (TV 2013-2017).

For more thoughts on this subject, read the Huffington Post article, Anatomy of the Female Anti-Hero by Lauren Duca.

WOMEN IN PRISON

WOMEN HANDLE PRISON differently than men, and often far better. If your story involves women behind bars, such as *Orange Is the New Black* (TV, 2013-present), *Chained Heat* (1983), or *Prisoner: Cell Block H* (TV, 1979-1986), you'd do well to read *In the Mix: Struggle and Survival in a Women's Prison* by Barbara Owen:

> ...Like most experiences, imprisonment and its subsequent response is a gendered one. ...[Female prison] culture develops in ways markedly different from the degradation, violence, and predatory structure of male prison life.
> —Barbara Owen, *In the Mix*

In the Mix covers everything you need to know about how prison conflict is resolved and relationships built, as well as the home and street life that sends women to prison, the difference between "inmates" and "convicts," how to gain and give respect, relationships with corrections officers, etc. For example, in one of Ms. Owen's many interviews, a prisoner revealed:

"If an officer raises his or her voice to you, some women are petrified. The fear from past abuse comes back and they are scared."

Most of the conflict in women's prison is verbal. The primary danger is not from violence, but manipulation. As one officer who worked in both male and female prisons put it:

"[Male prisoners] will try to game you but will give up. Women will continue over a much longer time; they are more patient, will work on you a little bit at a time… there is also the problem of sexual manipulation here. Females have natural resistance to seduction— males do not and it can get you in trouble…"

So it's not surprising that seventy percent of female prisoners prefer dealing with male staff. As one prisoner explained:

"We have learned to get around men with tears or flattery. None of that works on the female staff because they know it is bullshit."

FEMALE VILLAINS: PUTTING
LIPSTICK ON THE DEVIL

LIKE HEROES AND ANTI-HEROES, strong female villains should also find a home in your stories, but not as stereotypes. The success of any story relies on the strength of its villain.

Make sure your villains are interesting people struggling to solve interesting problems in interesting ways. Two great examples from classic films are Brigid O'Shaughnessy from *The Maltese Falcon* (1941) and Norma Desmond from *Sunset Boulevard* (1950). Both different, both dangerous! One sane, one insane. One young, one old. Both try to creatively problem solve in very female ways as opposed to the male villains in their films.

Villains come in two types: loners and those who either hide behind or act under the authority of a group. Female villains who wish to enact large-scale evil use groups, while those interested in smaller, more personal evil tend to go it alone.

Looking at this further, it seems likely that female villains acting in groups are charming and functional enough to be sociopaths, while those operating alone trend toward psychopaths—unless they are possessed of so much personal power they do not require the support of a group to enact their large-scale plans. Maleficent, the sorceress from *Sleeping Beauty* (1959) is one such example, and Jean Grey/Dark

Phoenix from *The Uncanny X-Men* comic book (issues #101-108, 1976-77 and #129-#138, 1980) is another.

FEMALE VILLAINS WHO USE GROUPS

- The Wicked Witch from *The Wizard of Oz* (1939) uses an army of men and flying monkeys
- Elizabeth Bathory from *Countess Dracula* (1971) uses her aristocratic position and estate
- Nurse Ratched from *One Flew Over the Cuckoo's Nest* (1975) uses her position of authority in a mental hospital
- Katherine Wentworth from *Dallas* (TV, 1978-1991) uses an oil company
- Alexis Carrington from *Dynasty* (TV, 1981-1989) also uses an oil company
- Angela Channing from *Falcon Crest* (TV, 1981-1990) uses a winery
- Diana from *V* (TV, 1984-85) uses an alien invasion force
- Nancy Downs from *The Craft* (1996) uses a coven of witches
- Regina George from *Mean Girls* (2004) uses a clique of rich girls
- Nina Myers from *24* (TV, 2001-2010) uses a federal counterterrorism agency
- Cersei Baratheon from *Game of Thrones* (TV, 2011-2018) uses an entire kingdom
- Mariah Dillard from *Luke Cage* (TV, 2016-present) uses her criminal and political connections

FEMALE VILLAINS WHO ACT ALONE

- Maleficent from *Sleeping Beauty* (1959)
- Carmilla Karnstein from *The Vampire Lovers* (1970)
- Evelyn from *Play Misty for Me* (1971)

- Margaret White from *Carrie* (1976)
- Pamela Voorhees from *Friday the 13th* (1980)
- Alex Forrest from *Fatal Attraction* (1987)
- Annie Wilkes from *Misery* (1990)
- Catherine Tramell from *Basic Instinct* (1992)
- Hedra Carlson from *Single White Female* (1992)
- Asami from *Audition* (1999)
- Samara from *The Ring* (2002)
- Esther from *Orphan* (2009)

HAIR, FASHION, MAKEUP: WOMEN'S CHAINS, WOMEN'S ARMOR

I SAVED this chapter for last because while it's important, it's the *least important* thing you need to know about writing realistic women. Just like the women in your life, what matters most is what's *inside* your female characters. Who they are, what they want. The rest is just window dressing.

Now that I've put this chapter in perspective, let's get started!

HAIR, fashion, makeup... We all know many women are obsessed with getting them "right," at least to some degree. Unlike men, who can just roll out of bed, throw on whatever's handy, and call it good, women can't. Well, they can, but they will be judged for it.

Harshly.

To avoid that judgment, many women will spend at least an hour or two getting ready to leave the house, and more time later if they intend to go somewhere special, like on a date or to a party. That adds up to a lot of hours staring into closets and mirrors.

Then, when they finally do go out, there's a ton of comparing themselves to other women going on. Women notice details men don't, from the exact shade of lipstick to the style of outfit to the brand of shoes. Men could care less, seeing only the broad strokes if they notice them at all.

The makeover is something every woman does sooner or later, often as a response to some setback or rejection. It can be subtle, but is often dramatic. The worse the situation, the more drastic the change. While your story may not call for such a scene, it will almost certainly call for some scene involving hair, fashion, and makeup.

As men writing about women, it's pretty much impossible for us to get all that stuff right. Even if we do a ton of research, we'll still get it wrong. Maybe not all of it, but enough to look stupid to female readers. So how do we solve that?

By avoiding it as much as possible.

My advice is not to sweat the details. It's too easy to get bogged down. Provide the bare minimum information and move on; you can get female friends, editors, or beta readers to fill in specific details later.

Here are some examples of hair, fashion, and makeup scenes from my upcoming vampire novel, *Forever Dark*. Each example provides just a few key details (vetted for accuracy by my female editor and beta readers).

Later that night, Naomi and I snuck a bottle of vodka from her mom's liquor cabinet to celebrate. We mixed it with fruit punch, got buzzed, then spent a couple hours playing with my hair and makeup. After all, if I looked good enough on the outside, maybe Scott would notice I wasn't so bad on the inside.

"That's it," Naomi said. "I think we've got it."

I studied myself in the mirror, turning this way and that in the black stretch minidress Naomi had bought for me. Was it enough?

"Relax," Naomi said. "Scott will take one look and instantly fall in love. He'll say, 'Oh my, you're too beautiful for words'! and just be all..." She exaggerated falling over backwards with one hand draped across her forehead, fake-fainting like in one of those old movies. She fluttered her eyelashes and sighed dramatically.

We both had a good laugh. And another drink.

"My turn," Naomi said. "I need some practice looking hot too."

We did her mahogany curls in an updo and set off her light brown eyes with some olive green eyeshadow. Her eyes really popped, the gold flecks standing out like glitter.

"You look totally sexified."

Naomi beamed, admiring herself in the mirror.

Note that I don't go on and on about every little thing; I focus on how the hair, fashion, and makeup make my characters *feel*. And feeling good is the whole reason women are so into all this stuff in the first place. It gives them a sense of power and control. They see it as armor, their first line of defense against a world that's stacked against them.

The next morning, Naomi's dad picked her up at noon. I was at the mall twenty minutes later, my Hello Kitty backpack full of everything I'd need for my date. I wandered around till I got bored. M·A·C gave free makeovers, so that seemed like a good way to kill time. When I got there, a heavily made-up brunette stood behind the counter.

"Hi," I said, "I'm going out with this new guy tonight, and I want to look really hot."

"No problem." The girl came around the counter and sat me in the makeover chair. "First, we have to get this old makeup off." She wiped a cleansing pad over my face, then applied base with a sponge and brushed on loose powder. "I'm going to add some primer to your lids to make the shadow really dark." She smudged charcoal-gray around my eyes, then pale silver highlighter on my brow bones. Liquid eyeliner and two coats of mascara followed. A matte lip finish completed the makeover.

"Well?" she asked. "What do you think? It's a whole new you, right?"

"Yeah, but I can't believe it! I never thought I could look this good."

> The M·A·C girl had erased my face and replaced it with something out of my dreams. It was ravishing. Unreal. A stranger's face, yet it was mine.

While that scene goes into a lot more detail, the rough draft went something like this: "Cindy goes to the mall to get a makeover. She now feels empowered to overcome her fear of disappointing Scott. Fill in details later." If I had tried to get that makeover scene perfect in my rough draft, it would have been a joke and my novel would never be finished. So I outsourced the details to my editor, then prettied it up later. The result is a realistic makeover scene written in my own voice.

Since I already have one fairly explicit makeover routine, when the time came for a second, I didn't waste time going into details again, just cut right to the end result:

> I did my hair in an updo fastened with rhinestone clips, then swung by M·A·C to get another free makeover. When it was done, I looked like a model. Between the makeup, the dress, and my powers, how could Scott resist?

That's a lot easier to write and still gets the point across. The reader already has the details from the previous makeover, so there's no point going into them again.

Here's an example of a bare bones hair and makeup routine. Again, note how I focus on how the ritual makes her *feel*. What she actually looks like is less important.

> I got ready for school, putting a lot of effort into my hair and makeup. When it was done, I looked amazing. Radiant. Glowing.

Up until now, the examples have dealt with looking good. Now let's take some time to explore what women go through when they're not looking their best:

I pulled down the vanity mirror and cringed at my tangled hair and bloody mouth, the darkly staring, hollow eyes. I wiped my mouth and chin with Kleenex from my purse, then aimed the heat vents at my hair, using my fingers to comb through the worst of the tangles. Once it was dry enough, I pointed the vents at my dress while I fixed my makeup. I popped a pair of mints, ignoring the oddly bitter flavor.

Eventually, the girl in the mirror resembled me. Enough to pass for human.

When a female character is not paying attention to her appearance, it may signify something is terribly wrong, as in the following example:

When I got to Naomi's, she answered the door wearing baggy sweats and no makeup.

"Sorry I took so long," I said. "I had to do some stuff for my mom."

"What the hell? You could have texted."

I apologized again as we went into the kitchen. She offered me a Diet Coke. I chugged it, hating the taste but needing the caffeine, then opened another.

Naomi watched me irritably. "Thirsty much? Come on, let's go to my room. My mom'll be home any minute, and we need to talk."

Note that Cindy (the POV character) does not acknowledge Naomi's disheveled appearance, but immediately recognizes her friend is in trouble. She immediately switches to apology mode, not wanting to upset her friend further, then waits for Naomi to tell her what's going on.

If this were a scene with two male characters, the first thing the POV guy might say would be like, "Dude! You look terrible," possibly followed by an affectionate insult or simple, "What's up?" But that's only if his buddy wasn't normally a slob, and if he even bothered to notice something was wrong in the first place.

Why the big difference? Because men favor blunt, direct communication, while women tend toward subtle, indirect communication (unless they're really angry). That's an important detail to understand if you want to get your female dialogue right.

LESSONS I'VE LEARNED WRITING CROSS-GENDER CHARACTERS

CROSS-GENDER WRITING DOESN'T HAVE to be hard—if you do your research. It also helps to get Beta readers, a close friend, and/or an editor of the opposite sex. That's what I did with my Young Adult novels and short stories, and it absolutely made me a better writer, and a better man.

In her reviews of my YA books, Melanie Marsh at Fang Freakin' Tastic Reviews says: "[Jackson Dean Chase] perfectly captures the feelings of being that awkward teen girl. I know because I was that girl," and "Jackson has a way with words that leaves me in awe of his understanding of the female psyche." These quotes were incredibly validating for me as a male author who (so far) exclusively writes female main characters and almost always in the first person.

I'm not saying I have a perfect understanding of the female psyche because as a man, that just isn't possible, just like it isn't possible for a woman to have a complete understanding of what it's like to be a man. *But it is possible to get close*—if you're willing to do the work and immerse yourself in how men think. Consume their fiction, their movies and TV. See not only what they respond to, but *how* they respond. Men and women are different genders, not different species. You'll be surprised how much is the same.

I can't recall who first said it, but I like to keep this quote in mind: "Men and women want pretty much the same things—women just like to talk about them more."

ROLE-PLAYING GAMES

Another trick—and one I recommend highly—is to play characters of the opposite sex in pen and paper role-playing games (RPGs) like *Dungeons & Dragons*, *Star Wars*, *Call of Cthulhu*, etc.

You should be looking to join a group that plays a game in the same or similar genre(s) you write in. Multiple RPGs exist for just about any genre or subgenre you can think of: fantasy, horror, hard-boiled/noir, sci-fi, secret agents, steampunk, superheroes, etc. The problem isn't finding a game, it's picking one!

With the right group, you can quickly and easily immerse yourself in what it's like to not be you *or* your gender. It's like acting, but interactive storytelling you make up as you go along. You and the other players each take on the role of a single character within the world, while the Game Master takes on the role of everyone else (the NPCs, or "non-player characters").

Particularly shocking for me within the game world were the constant unwelcome advances and insults my female character endured from male NPCs, along with the frequent inability to be heard, respected, or understood by them. I was viewed as a "support unit" rather than a hero, and had to work twice as hard to be recognized as one. It was extremely challenging, but ultimately rewarding.

Aside from immersing myself in female pop culture and psychology, I credit role-playing with giving me the biggest leg up when it came time to write female-driven fiction.

You can often find gaming groups recruiting new players at your local comic book shop. Ask the owner or check the bulletin board. It may help to explain you're an author trying to achieve better cross-gender writing by experiencing what it's like to be a male hero. Who knows? You may get some extra beta readers—and fans—from the group!

AFTERWORD

I'm profoundly grateful to the writers who made this book possible, and to all the women—*especially my editor*—who shared their amazing advice and stories while helping me whip this project into shape.

Honestly, I'm not sure why a lot of the stuff we've learned here isn't taught in school. Demystifying gender differences and breaking down barriers (real and imagined) would go a long way toward creating a better world for all of us, and certainly, better relationships.

Happy Writing,
Jackson Dean Chase

Get a free book at
www.JacksonDeanChase.com

BIBLIOGRAPHY

FOR HOW TO WRITE REALISTIC WOMEN

FICTION

- *The Bitch Posse* by Martha O'Connor

NONFICTION

- *45 Master Characters* by Victoria Lynn Schmidt
- *Daring Greatly: How the Courage to Be Vulnerable Transforms the Way We Live, Love, Parent, and Lead* by Brené Brown
- *In the Mix: Struggle and Survival in a Women's Prison* by Barbara Owen
- *Queen Bees & Wannabes: Helping Your Daughter Survive Cliques, Gossip, Boyfriends, and the New Realities of Girl World* by Rosalind Wiseman
- *Reviving Ophelia: Saving the Selves of Adolescent Girls* by Mary Pipher, Ph.D.
- *The Virgin's Promise: Writing Stories of Feminine Creative, Spiritual, and Sexual Awakening* by Kim Hudson

- *The Writer's Journey: Mythic Structure for Writers* by Christopher Vogler

MEMOIR

- *Loose Girl: A Memoir of Promiscuity* by Kerry Cohen

TESTS AND ARTICLES (Google 'em!)

- Anatomy of the Female Anti-Hero by Lauren Duca
- The Bechdel Test
- 10 Ways to Spot A Manic Pixie Dream Girl
- The Mary Sue Test

WHAT'S NEXT?

NOW THAT YOU'VE MASTERED story hooks and character creation, it's time to move on to *The Ultimate Author's Guide Omnibus 2* which contains everything you need to know about writing science fiction, fantasy, and horror. Inside, you'll find two more of my guides:

- *Writing Monsters & Maniacs* covers a broad range of alien and fantasy races, killer robots and other machines, as well as all your favorite monsters and psycho killers. It includes 150 plot ideas plus tons of suggested movies and TV shows.

- *Writing Apocalypse & Survival* takes you into the apocalyptic and post-apocalyptic genres, giving you complete, infinitely expandable plot templates as well everything you need to know about what happens when the world ends. The book covers zombies, *Mad Max*-style road warriors, and more.

If you need help describing things—and I do mean anything—than be sure and grab my *Writers' Phrase Books*:

- #1 Horror

- #2 Post-Apocalypse
- #3 Action
- #4 Fantasy
- #5 Fiction (a short series sampler)
- #6 Science Fiction
- #7 Romance, Emotion, and Erotica

Note that the phrase books are intended as standalones, so all but the Romance one repeat a lot of the same action descriptions. You may not need to own more than one or two of these phrase books.

That's all till next time. Thank you for buying my book and I hope to see you again soon.

— JACKSON DEAN CHASE
Get a free book at
www.JacksonDeanChase.com

P.S.: If you enjoyed this omnibus, please leave a review to help others on their author journey.

ABOUT JACKSON DEAN CHASE

JACKSON DEAN CHASE is a USA TODAY bestselling author and award-winning poet. His fiction has been praised as "irresistible" in *Buzzfeed* and "diligently crafted" in *The Huffington Post*. Jackson's books on writing fiction have helped thousands of authors.

FROM THE AUTHOR: "I've always loved science fiction, fantasy, and horror, but it wasn't until I combined them with pulp thrillers and *noir* that I found my voice as an author. I want to leave my readers breathless, want them to feel the same desperate longing, the same hope and fear my heroes experience as they struggle not just to survive, but to become something more." — JDC

www.JacksonDeanChase.com
jackson@jacksondeanchase.com

amazon.com/author/jacksondeanchase

bookbub.com/authors/jackson-dean-chase

facebook.com/jacksondeanchaseauthor

instagram.com/jacksondeanchase

twitter.com/Jackson_D_Chase

Made in the USA
Las Vegas, NV
10 January 2022

41025182R00173